HOW TO INFLUENCE PEOPLE

A Guide to Develop Mind Control Techniques, Learn how to Win Friends and Influence Other People, Discover the Secret to Defend Yourself from Brainwashing and Deception

J.R. Smith

© Copyright 2019 by J.R. Smith - All rights reserved.

This book is provided with the sole purpose of providing relevant information on a specific topic for which every reasonable effort has been made to ensure that it is both accurate and reasonable. Nevertheless, by purchasing this book you consent to the fact that the author, as well as the publisher, are in no way experts on the topics contained herein, regardless of any claims as such that may be made within. As such, any suggestions or recommendations that are made within are done so purely for entertainment value. It is recommended that you always consult a professional prior to undertaking any of the advice or techniques discussed within.

This is a legally binding declaration that is considered both valid and fair by both the Committee of Publishers Association and the American Bar Association and should be considered as legally binding within the United States.

The reproduction, transmission, and duplication of any of the content found herein, including any specific or extended information will be done as an illegal act regardless of the end form the information ultimately takes. This includes copied versions of the work both physical, digital and audio unless express consent of the Publisher is provided beforehand. Any additional rights reserved.

Furthermore, the information that can be found within the pages described forthwith shall be considered both accurate and truthful when it comes to the recounting of facts. As such, any use, correct or incorrect, of the provided information will render the Publisher free of responsibility as to the actions taken outside of their direct purview. Regardless, there are zero scenarios where the original author or the Publisher can be deemed liable in any fashion for any damages or hardships that may result from any of the information discussed herein.

Additionally, the information in the following pages is intended only for informational purposes and should thus be thought of as universal. As befitting its nature, it is presented without assurance regarding its prolonged validity or interim quality. Trademarks that are mentioned are done without written consent and can in no way be considered an endorsement from the trademark holder.

Table of Contents

Introduction 1
Chapter 1: The principles of persuasion 3
Chapter 2: Difference between influence and manipulation 10
Chapter 3: The tools and techniques used to influence 17
Chapter 4: Explain how the environment affects our brain development 27
Chapter 5: Communication skills improvement and influence 32
Chapter 6: How to use empathy for better communication and influence other people 40
Chapter 7: Tips to help people become a better friend, a better parent, a better partner, better businessman or women, outlining the beliefs or mental habits that one person should cultivate to use successful negotiation methods in daily life situations. 47
Chapter 8: Influence in dating and relationships 56
Chapter 9: Influence of friendship 67
Chapter 10: Influence in parenting 71
Chapter 11: Influence at workplace 75
Chapter 12: Influence in advertising 82
Chapter 13: Influence on religion 90
Chapter 14: Provide knowledge ethically dealing with other people's emotions. 97
Chapter 15: Tips and checklist to spot and stop manipulators. 104
Chapter 16: How to detect deception 112
Chapter 17: Tips and workout to increase self-esteem in order to avoid being manipulated 118
Chapter 18: Illustrations of manipulation and ways of defending against it 130
Chapter 19: Guide to dealing with bullying behavior 137
Conclusion 141
Description 142

Introduction

Most of us want to influence people around us and beyond. Influencing people may have appeared as a forte reserved for some people but the entry of this book will systematically guide you. In a highly structured and informative manner, the reader is introduced to the principles of persuasion, the difference between influence and manipulation as well as the tools and techniques used to influence. A reader is walked through how the environment impacts brain development to help appreciate why some people may be vulnerable to manipulation while others are good influencers. Since manipulation and influence relates to interacting with people, the environment plays a significant role in how one navigates manipulation as well as influence. As expected, the book underscores the role of communication skills in accomplishing influence.

Additionally, the book explores what constitutes empathy and its critical role in communicating effectively. The other interesting area that the author explores is providing tips to help people become a better friend, a better parent, better partner, better businessman or women, outlining the beliefs or mental habits that one person should cultivate to use successful negotiation methods in daily life situations. Another topic that most people will find useful concerns ways of exerting influence on dating and relationships, exerting influence in friendship, and exerting influence in parenting. Most of us want to exert influence at the workplace, which can increase our life chances, and for this reason; the author dedicated an entire chapter to help the reader learn ways of exerting influence at the workplace.

Chapter 1: The principles of persuasion

Most people would wish to influence others. Influence is the least cost and yet effective ways to make masses of people obey your wishes where the wishes are meant to mutually benefit all. Influence can be inborn or learned as a skill or both. Think of wooing voters without having to spend significant sums of money to sway them. Imagine a situation where you sway the management to buy into your ideas and drop their hardline stance. While all these appear reserved for certain people, it is possible to accomplish influence by exploring and integrating the Robert Cialdini principles of influence.

Reciprocity

The fundamental principle of influence is to simply grant that which you want to receive. In other terms, doing right by others is a great way to make them return that favor. The principle of reciprocity is a potent one. Reciprocity can be expressed in multiple ways such as giving others small gifts, doing favors for those in need, and treating others with respect and are all things that can earn you points with other individuals. For this reason, a recommended approach is to always help others and remain kind when they have an opportunity, as there is likelihood that you will need their help in the future. It is these small acts of kindness that will be remembered and become useful when one needs a favor.

Consistency

Regarding the principle of consistency, it is anchored on the power of active and voluntary commitments that leads to people abiding by their word. For this reason, let us explore these requirements in a detailed manner. The first aspect is an active commitment and by active it implies that something that is written or spoken to other people. The start of persuasion is making people say that they will do a particular thing. When an individual commits to something then they are much more likely to follow through. The next step is to make the declaration public. If other people witness the commitment, then the level of accountability is likely to be enhanced and in most cases, no one wants to retract. Lastly, the commitment has to be voluntary because if you force someone to make an active and public commitment that they did not decide on themselves then you will have accomplished nothing.

Social proof

We rely on social cues from others on how to think, feel and act in different situations. Peers lead in an exhibition of social proof among the general population. Social proof then refers to a person depending on social cues from others on how to think, act and feel in different situations. Against this backdrop, one is likely to use a particular intern in their department to influence other interns by first orienting the selected intern to ideal attributes. When other interns see another employee like themselves, they are likely to mimic or adapt to that behavior. It is thus important to get one of the target people to exhibit the desired action or attributes to influence the others.

Liking

Most people prefer those individuals that like them or who view them as friends. Although simple, this is a powerful concept. We can use the principle of liking in several ways. First, one can find common ground with the individuals he or she meets. If one can connect with such people on their interests or hobbies then one will have promising ground to start from. One should be observant of people to notice any clues that may make one discover shared understanding. The second means of inviting the liking of another person is to make genuine praise. Praise that is exaggerated is considered a flatter and somehow dishonest. However, paying compliments and being charming can help one build a positive rapport with other people. One mustn't overdo paying compliments. For emphasis, the praise accorded to the target individual should be genuine.

Authority

If people perceive you as an authority in an area then they are likely to defer to you. Most people consider experts as capable of giving shorter but effective approaches to complex issues that would see other people take longer to accomplish. Against this backdrop, one should seek to establish the credibility of authority and expertise before seeking to influence the target masses. Most people miss this window of opportunity since they assume that others will notice their expertise automatically. For this reason, you should explicitly make the target audience aware of your expertise. Authority can be established in several ways. For instance, make all your academic credentials and awards visible to your target audience. Authority can be established by making short anecdotes as well as background information shared in casual conversations. For emphasis, your expertise is not always a known quantity and one should convey it when the chance presents.

Scarcity

Expectedly, people value what is rare or scarce. Nothing strange as this perfectly satisfies the law of supply and demand because as things become scarce, they become more valuable to others. The principle of scarcity can be applied to convince others. One approach is to make offers limited-time, limit supply, or one-time with creates a perception of scarcity. How one presents such opportunities counts in that if one focuses more on loss language then the message becomes more potent. Then there is the exclusivity approach which concerns granting access to services, information, or other items to a limited set of people elucidating a sense of exclusiveness. The goal is to get the target audience to translate all these as a favor extended to them or that you are valuing them more than others. If one combines all of the above approaches then his or her powers of influence will significantly increase.

Illustrations

When one goes beyond the expectations when dealing with another person then the person is offering more than needed. Human beings are rational and will promptly notice that they have been given more care or service than should be the norm. By offering more than expected, you are taking the lead of the current and future interactions with the target person. Most human beings have learned to offer back in equal measure when they get extra care and concern from others. The overall aim of the principle of reciprocity is that it makes the other person feel that they owe you for what you did to them even when not asking for it. By being generous with empathy, concern and physical gifts you are chaining the target person to concede more in future interactions. Through reciprocity, you build trust and propagate the relationship.

Regarding, the principle of scarcity, people are drawn to that which is difficult to find as it is considered rare, exclusive and unique. Scarcity motivates an individual to make the best use of the limited opportunity. Have you ever wondered why most politicians will maintain their presence minimum even when they have no justification to appear briefly? The reason for this is that scarcity makes the target entertain the perception that the individual is highly valued and his or her appearance should be appreciated. All these developments increase the eagerness to listen and believe the politician. On a personal level, if your partner or spouse suddenly withdraws chances are that you are likely to want to feel their presence more. The art of limiting your availability helps enhance your value as a person as well as your opinions and a good influencer creates the perception that he or she is highly sought after.

For the principle of authority, people tend to coalesce around figures of authority and this is the primary motivation for using celebrities to endorse products. Companies spend significantly to get a celebrity or a recognizable sporting personality to endorse their product because the target masses view the celebrity as an authority in that domain. In formal contexts, figures of authority may include accomplished engineers, doctors, and journalists whose opinion is seen being the most applicable option. Fortunately, the principle of authority allows any person to create the perception of authority and get the target audience actively listening and implementing what he or she says. As indicated, one should start by making the audience aware of your credentials to enhance your credibility. One can also use memorization to make the audience feel that the individual is well furnished with the target area.

Relatedly, ensuring that you are consistent is important as it helps carve out the image that you are aware of yourself and are principled. No one would want to follow an individual that switches sides during an argument or a crisis. People appreciate consistent people and are likely to believe them even when earlier on they dismissed such people. There are chances that you voted for a political candidate that appeared to have a stand even there were sufficient factors to make you reconsider your views. Take a look at most adverts of a particular product; they try to maintain consistency concerning the utility that the product provides to the end consumer. For instance, try to review the adverts about Dettol soap and you will realize consistent is sustained. The other benefit of creating consistency is that it makes your target audience associate specific values with you even in contexts where you are not present.

Then there is the principle of consensus and a leader that allows for compromise can illustrate this. Chances are that you find a leader that is willing to strike a middle ground during conflicts as an understanding and humane leader. Compromise helps create the impression that one is understanding and can relate to how you are feeling. People tend to find persons that exhibit ideal human qualities such as empathy as honest.

Chapter 2: Difference between influence and manipulation

Expectedly, the influence that is misused for selfish gains qualifies to be manipulation. Manipulation is the deliberate application of influence for your gain at the expense of others while influence seeks to promote greater good by helping herd people in a particular direction. For instance, if you want people to drop certain cultural practices that are retrogressive then you will employ tactics that will make them believe your views. However, if you use the stated techniques to convince people to make them unknowingly help you attain your interests then that is manipulation. Overall, the primary difference between influence and manipulation is the motivation for convincing people.

Illustration

What is its influence?
Assume that Brian is at a restaurant with friends and after finishing the meal, he pays the bill for everyone without asking anyone to do it. Assume that Brian does this a couple of times. The next time Brian and friends go to a restaurant again, someone else foots the bill without asking others to chip in. In this manner, Brian has influenced others to follow his habit even though nonverbally.

What is manipulation?

Again, assume that Brian is at a restaurant with friends and just before the bill is brought, Brian pretends to be checking his pockets and says that he forgot his wallet. Brian does this a couple of times and no one asks Brian to foot the bill anymore. In this manner, Brian manipulated his friends to stop considering asking him to foot the bill.

For this context, the negative influence is manipulation. It is possible to influence people to do something that will harm or negatively affect them. For instance, you can influence your colleagues to elect a workplace leader who is ineffective because you dislike the company. In this case, your hatred for the organization has made you employ techniques of persuasion to make your colleagues elect an individual that will not perform to expectations. You have driven people to make a decision that will negatively affect their future at the organization just to satisfy your dislike of the organization. The rest of your colleagues are unaware that you were not genuine when urging them to vote in the current leader.

Additionally, with manipulation one is aggressive and will not allow the persuasion to develop gradually because of selfish intent. Influence is genuine and one is likely to allow it to manifest naturally but with manipulation, one wants to exploit the slim chance to realize selfish interests. For instance, a manipulator will exploit the fact that there is going to be a change in leadership at the organization and advance his influence to make workers vote in the least deserving leader. The motivation for influencing others to make an unwise decision is to ensure that the organization has little chance of getting effective feedback about the welfare of the employees and eventually face a mass exodus of resignations.

Relatedly, manipulation depends significantly on reading and exploiting body language while influence relies more on verbal cues of communication. For one to effectively manipulate people, he or she has to evoke appropriate facial expressions, tone of voice, posture, eye contact, and paralinguistic techniques. In other terms, manipulation requires timing for it to succeed while influence is less restricted and verbal cues of communication are enough to accomplish persuasion.

Unlike influence, a person manipulating others will feel dishonest and selfish if others found that he or she deliberately persuaded them. While both influence and manipulation may be subtle, a manipulator fears being exposed. A person seeking to influence others is comfortable should he or she be exposed since the persuasion is meant for mutual wellbeing of those affected. Unlike a person seeking to influence, a manipulator continuously seeks to sustain the status quo once he or she manages to control the target people.

Additionally, an influencer seeks to sway each person in the target audience whereas a manipulator focuses on simply attaining the selfish goal through persuasion. When manipulating people the intention is to simply attain your target goal and not to persuade each of the affected people. For this reason, once the manipulator feels that his or her plan is on track then the individual will not consider other people that are not impacted by the manipulation. A manipulator tends to get interested only in individuals capable of exposing the selfish intent of the manipulator and for this reason; a manipulator differentiates the audience to manage it. On the other hand, an influencer seeks to win everybody to his or her side and is not scared of dissenting voices.

One can also view manipulation as seeking to make the job of the manipulator easier while making the affected job harder. In some circumstances, a manipulator exploits others to enable him or she has an easy time while the affected people face difficulties executing their mandate. In such circumstances, manipulation seeks to dim the performance of others while elevating the perpetrator's performance. A manipulator in this context seeks to attract all the attention to his or her direction and exhibits sadistic attributes.

More illustration

Think of a student leader that breaks the code of conduct in a university. The student leader knows that he or she will face the disciplinary committee with the possibility of being suspended or expelled from the learning institution. However, the student leader understands that he or she commands significant support among the students and a section of the staff at the learning institution. The student leader then chooses to exploit the fact that a lot of students and a section of the staff will listen and believe his assertions and whips up the emotion of students and some of the staff. All these developments help precipitate a crisis at the learning institution making it difficult for the administration of the university to hold the student leader accountable for the violation of the code of conduct. In this case, the student leader is a manipulator. A manipulator avoids accountability when cornered and instead prefers to precipitate a crisis.

Now assume that the student leader is exposed as having used his influence among the students and a section of the staff to shield himself from disciplinary action. Chances are that the student leader would feel like a fraud and the affected would feel used for selfish gains. Again, the student leader cared not for anyone except for his interests a high likelihood. For instance, the student leader cared not for the implication if some students are let go without accounting for their misbehavior at the institution.

Another illustration of manipulation concerns the case of Alex who loathes the administration of his organization and yearns to make them feel cornered. Even though Alex puts on a face of a composed and disciplined employee, he is not. It happens that one unfortunate day, one of the workers is attacked by the security dogs in the compound of the organization. Alex then sees a rare opportunity to turn the workers against the management. So Alex whips up the emotion of employees and makes them feel that they are insecure and their welfare not adequately taken care of. The colleagues of Alex innocently believe that Alex's views are genuine and meant to help elevate their safety at precincts of the organization. From this illustration, Alex is a manipulator who takes advantage of an emotive situation to accomplish his interests devoid of the interests of the majority.

Again, Alex most likely cared not for the welfare of others but only his. Alex is not bothered about the reputation or longevity of the organization and its impact on the workers. In other words, if the organization was forced to suspend operations and laid-off workers then Alex would not be bothered that his colleagues are jobless. For Alex, as long his selfish interest triumphs then nothing else matters. Alex would also feel unease and ashamed if his selfish interest was exposed in all these developments.

On the other hand, influence can be demonstrated by Sharon's determination to make the community safe by having parents get actively involved in the lives of their teenagers. At first, Sharon realizes that few people are listening to her campaign to make parents more involved in the lives of their teenagers. Sharon then resorts to persuasion tactics by making the community notice her profession as a psychologist and gives them respect and attention to which they reciprocate. Sharon consistently communicates her message and campaign across the neighborhoods of the community and goes further to use one of the mothers actively involved in the life of her teenagers as an example. With time, the entire neighborhood sways to the message of Sharon. All these development indicate influence, which is the deliberate persuasion of people to align with your message and intentions for mutual gain.

Chapter 3: The tools and techniques used to influence

Conventional tools used to influence

There are various techniques and tools used to persuade people. The variety of techniques and tools employed to convince people to enable one to adjust persuasion tactics depending on the environment and the target audience. It can be argued that different tactics to influence an audience will vary depending on their age, level of education, place, ethnicity and religious affiliations. Conventional tools refer to widely acceptable methods and techniques to persuade people. These tools are conventional in that they elicit the least ethical protest on their usage. In this chapter, we are going to present the specific tools and techniques used to influence.

Logical persuading

Using this technique, one employs logic to explain what they want or believe in. Using logic to persuade is a fundamental tool to appeal to people. Logical persuading is widely practiced and is effective but it does not work for every person. In this technique, the influencer makes the target audience appreciate the suggested direction as the most reasonable, efficient and safe. Once the target audience has bought this line, they will in turn act as mini-influencers by recruiting more people to the suggested line of thought. Logical persuading is widely used by political leaders especially when seeking to unseat the incumbent. In conflict resolution, logical persuading as a technique tends to deliver.

Legitimizing

Legitimizing implies appealing to authority. Legitimizing is the least-effective technique to influence. One of the reasons for this technique is ineffective is that it takes attention away from the speaker and grants it to a recognizable authority. For this reason, appealing to authority may appear as an attempt to intimidate the audience. The second reason for this technique showing ineffectiveness is that it makes the target audience aware of the attempt to manipulate them. Consequently, the audience invokes the defense mechanism against explicit manipulation. However, legitimizing as a technique will work for most people and can elicit quick compliance especially in the formal settings.

Exchanging

In this context, exchanging techniques entails mediating or trading for cooperation and is most efficient when it is contained. In some circumstances, exchanging or compromise is the best way to persuade an audience. A shrewd influencer will create a perception of a standoff or crisis and offer the audience compromise which elevates the liking for the influencer. The underlying principle of the exchanging as a technique is to enable the participants to feel involved and appreciated rather than be passive participants. In conflict resolution and business negotiation, exchanging as a technique is widely preferred. However, using exchanging techniques should be limited to deserving contexts lest it qualifies as manipulation.

Stating

The technique of stating asserts what you want or believe. It is one of the persuading tools and most sufficient when one is self-confident and states ideas with an imperative tone of voice. In this technique of influence, one simply makes the audience aware of what he or she wants. In some contexts such as the church and school, this technique of influence works. Concerning power relations, stating as technique works where the target audience has no negotiating power when placed against the influencer. For instance, a principal of a school informing students on the need to keep time and submit homework constitutes an application of the stating technique of influencing. Stating can cause resistance if overused. The resistance to stating, as a technique is that it can create the impression that the rest of the audience is expected to align with the influencer and that they do not have the freedom to differ.

Socializing

The technique of socializing concerns getting to know the other person and being open and friendly. It is about finding common ground. Socializing involves complimenting people and making them feel good about themselves. Socializing is a critical influence on power tools and is widely applicable across different settings. Most politicians employ socializing by reducing themselves to the routine life of their voters which makes them relatable and believable. Ever thought why most political candidates during campaigns freely interact with the common man and even ride bicycles? The reason for this is that they are trying to socialize by appearing open and friendly.

Appealing to the relationship

The technique of appealing to relationship involves cooperating with people that you already know well premised on the length and strength of the actual relationships. The appealing to the relationship as a technique to influence is among the most effective persuasion tools. Creating a relationship enables to create a lasting influence as the participants feel that they owe the influence of cooperation and reciprocation. Think of why teachers invest significant mental energy in helping a connection with students. The reason for investing in a relationship is that the target individual readily accepts the persuasion as he or she imagines that the interaction is mutual and considerate of the welfare of the affected person.

Consulting

Stimulating or engaging people by asking questions constitutes a consulting technique. The consulting technique requires involving people in the solution or problem. The technique functions well with sharp and self-confident people that have a strong urge to devote ideas. People are likely to cooperate if they are made to feel that they matter and this is the logic behind consulting as a technique to influence. At the school level, the school administration will always involve student leaders even when it is clear that the school administration will not budge even if the student leaders disagree. The practice of involving the target audience helps lower resistance and enhances cooperation.

Building alliance

Alliance building involves creating formations to help impact other people through peer pressure or herd mentality. Even though alliance building is not invoked often, in some circumstances it is the most effective tool. For instance, most political contexts may invoke building alliances as a tool to influence. The other benefit of building alliances is that it allows one to have a sort of backup to the attempts to influence. The members of the alliance that you built will carry the burden of your influence which helps spread the persuasion as well as shield you should the target audience get dissatisfied with your efforts.

Appealing to values

The technique of making an emotional appeal involves invoking what people celebrate, respect and adhere to as a society or community. For instance, spiritual leaders will draw attention to values that build up the specific religion and to which the congregation identifies with. As such, the audience will quickly understand the authority and power wielded by the spiritual leader. A politician will appeal to the dominant religious, cultural and national values that the country identifies with which helps charm the audience. An idealist will make an emotional appeal to the audience to desire the envisioned perfect society. Business leaders may make an emotional appeal by drawing the attention of the audience to environmental degradation and influence the audience to embrace green technology products.

Modeling

In this technique, one behaves in a manner that he or she wants others to behave. Modeling as a means to influence can be accomplished by teaching, coaching, mentoring, and counseling. The benefit of modeling is that the audience is largely unaware that they are being guided to align with the wishes of the speaker. Leaders, parents, managers, and public figures influence others via modeling all the time. For instance, if your mothers show you how to dress by dressing well then she is setting the example and in the process influencing. On the other hand, you are unknowingly trying to be like your mother not knowing that your mother intentionally sought to influence you.

Controversial influencing tactics

The controversial techniques to influence include avoidance, manipulation, intimidation, and issuing threats. These techniques are treated as negative because they deny the target audience the legitimate right to speak their will. The target audience is forced to adhere to something as opposed to their best interests. Think of your school days, or the experience when you were arrested and locked in a police cell. There are instances where the controversial influence tactics may work such as a prosecutor seeking the cooperation of the accused or where a teacher wants to quickly restore order in the school and prevent chaos. Controversial influencing tactics should be used in moderation and in extreme circumstances such as averting chaos.

Avoiding

Avoidance entails forcing others to act and in most cases opposed to their best interests by dodging accountability or dispute. In this technique, rather than individual leading others to confront their challenges, he or she selectively approach the issue to elicit the highest level of cooperation. For this reason, avoidance as a technique buries any issue that can disrupt the status quo of society and focuses on what the author finds satisfying. In a way, avoidance is related to appeasing where emotive issues are overlooked and the influencer concentrates on what people desire to hear.

Manipulating

In manipulation, one seeks to influence through deceit, lies, swindles, and hoaxes. Hiding your real intention or deliberately withholding information others need to arrive at the right conclusion is manipulation. In manipulation, the individual seeks to use the masses to accomplish selfish gains at the expense of others. Bullies and tyrants prefer intimidation.

Threatening

Issuing threats lest they comply and making examples of some people so others understand that the threats are real. Issuing threats is widely used by tyrants and dictators. In most cases, threats help attain short-term compliance but in the absence of close supervision, the target individuals quickly let go of the modified behavior and perceptions. Think of your early school days, there are chances that you were issued with threats that made you and others readily comply but as soon as you realized that, you can navigate the consequences the threats no longer counted.

In some cases, managers or supervisors may issue threats, especially where the employees are resisting change. A supervisor may threaten employees that those that do not learn to use the new system may face forced early retirement. In this context, the employees will buy into the recommendations of the supervisor due to the potency of the threats issued.

Sanctions

Through this technique, the individual issues sanctions, which are well-calculated restrictions that create uneasiness on the target. Sanctions force the affected person to feel emotional, social, personal and economic pressure to which the person blames himself or herself. Sanctions may involve influencer banning or making it difficult for others to transact with you. At the global stage, economic sanctions help exert control over the targeted country. If a country receives sanctions then it is deliberately denied trade partners which elevate negative publicity of the country. A real-life example is how the United States uses sanctions to contain other emerging economic powers that do not cooperate with the United States.

Information control

Filtering information can elevate one over others. Multiple contexts make people desperate for information. It is one reason why media houses wield influence. However, when practicing information control, it is necessary to uphold consistency. The other effect of information control is that it makes the individual be perceived as being connected, knowledgeable and powerful which enhances the influence that he or she wields. Due to the proliferation of social media, withholding information may not always work as people can still access the much-needed information from independent influencers.

Image management

In this context, image management includes the character, personality, grooming and diction of an individual. Your style and consistency of dressing affect how people perceive you. Additionally, a certain form of dressing may communicate nonconformity or gentleness. Similarly, the choice of words by a person will determine the reception and reaction of the target audience. Our character may make us find it easier or difficult to influence others. Concerning personality, our personality rarely changes compared to character. For this reason, one should define their personality and use the patch up the shortcomings when attempting to influence.

Chapter 4: Explain how the environment affects our brain development

The environment entails people, physical surroundings, culture, and societal order prevalent around an individual. The personality, presence, and character of people around a child affect the brain development of the child. The state of the physical surroundings in terms of quality of air, water, and aesthetics impacts the development of a child. The culture that one is raised in will also affect brain development as well as the societal order.

First, growing up in institutional care may qualify as a deprived environment and affects brain development. Institutional care is linked to brain deficits. A deprived environment implies that one misses out on certain psychological, physical and societal aspects of life. Children raised in institutional care are likely to lack adequate caregiver personal attention such as touch and play. All these developments affect the growth of the baby. The institutional environment is likely to lack the natural variance of factors that are an inherent presence in homes such as attention from other family members, access to different adults and changing sites for care such as the lawn, rooms and uninterrupted floor space for a baby.

Additionally, higher parental educational and economic statuses can enhance the brain development of a child, especially concerning learning and memory. Children that grow up in an environment of abundance are likely to have good nutritional options, less stressing environment and adequate presence of parents in their lives. On the other hand, children that are raised in low economic status families are likely to receive care from parents juggling between several low paying jobs that are stressful. Such parents are likely to offer basic nutrition options to their children. Activities that may enhance learning and memory are more manifest with parents that possess high educational and economic status.

Relatedly, children exposed to stress and abuse show enhanced stress response. Adults with enhanced brain reactions to stressors are prone to physical and mental health problems. Correspondingly, adults that grew up in poverty exhibited high memory deficit incidences compared to others from different economic backgrounds. Early exposure to stressors makes a child internalize reaction to stress as part of human being growth. Since these stressors are activated at the early stage of the child development in this context, the child grows up exhibiting increased stress reactions to triggers of stress. In adult life, the person may develop physical and emotional health problems linked to stressors that he or she should not.

Outside the context of the United States, culture affects brain development in different ways. For instance, some cultures restrict the diet that a child can be fed on. Little consideration may be accorded on the effect of withdrawing certain feeds given to a child. As such, certain cultural practices may deny a child the requisite nutritive minerals and vitamins necessary for healthy brain growth. Additionally, certain cultural practices bar a mother taking her child in the open and this can influence the brain development of the child. Certain cultural practices may limit the number, kind of individuals that help take care of the baby, and this may imply that a baby is stuck with an underperforming caregiver. All these developments affect the mental health of a baby especially brain development.

On the extreme, the physical environment may expose a baby to harmful chemicals such as smoke, contaminated water, contaminated food, and cigarette smoke. Lead contamination has been shown to negatively affect the brain development of babies and if one is residing in areas where the water contains lead then the baby's brain development will be affected. Similarly, a baby exposed to pollutants such as smoke may have its growth negatively impacted. Contaminated food may increase allergic reactions from a baby, which may lead to the baby missing out on the daily-recommended nutritional intake. In this manner, the physical environment can directly affect the baby.

For instance, babies that are raised in slums or projects tend to exhibit a broad spectrum of mental defects and mental health defects. First, such babies may miss out on basic healthcare such as immunization due to difficulties of the parents accessing healthcare services or due to ignorance that makes such parents shun programs such as immunization. Babies in slums tend to lack requisite nutrition, which can negatively affect their mental growth. Parents residing in slums are juggling multiple low paying jobs, which leave little time to show parental care and play with a baby, which can affect the mental health of such a baby.

However, there are numerous causes of a baby exhibiting good brain development irrespective of the financial status of the parents. There is a possibility of parents in high-income areas not according a baby adequate attention that is necessary for the good health of the baby. Holding the baby and touching the baby is necessary for reassurance and perception of love, which ultimately affects the mental health of a baby. A parent in a high-income neighborhood that uses drugs and smokes may negatively impact the growth of her baby.

Concerning scientific evidence, several scientific articles affirm that stressful environments affect the size and quality of brain matter. These studies imply that a child born and being raised in a slum or project is likely not to realize full brain development was the child to be in an environment of abundance. The contributing factors to this development include access to nutrition choices, access to healthcare, a parent that is less stressed and access to props that enhance mental development as well as residing in less polluted areas.

While we have explored the different ways that the environment impacts brain development, it is important to remember that a significant part of brain development is determined by genetics and the health of the individual. Much of the brain development is largely mediated and moderated by genetic makeup that we inherit from our parents. Then there is the health that one has at birth and the first year, which affects brain development. Babies unfortunate to have health problems at birth are likely to exhibit brain development challenges.

Chapter 5: Communication skills improvement and influence

Communication skills refer to verbal and nonverbal competencies that make the exchange of message effective. While some people are born gifted communicators, a majority of people have to learn communication skills to enable them to accomplish a social transaction. Even for individuals that are gifted communicators, they have to learn communication skills due to the diversity of audiences. If one aspires to influence people communication skills is the critical success factor in this endeavor. A common mistake we make is to assume that we possess the requisite communication skills. Most people without adequate communication wrongly believe that they possess the requisite communication skills.

While most people acknowledge the criticality of communication skills, few commit to learn and practice communication skills. Relatedly, nonverbal communication is highly critical in communication yet widely ignored when horning communication skills. Body language, which is essentially nonverbal communication, affects the quality and quantity of communication. In this chapter, we will explore requisite communication skills and make a connection to how they can enhance one in influencing others.

Empathy

In this context, showing empathy requires one to place themselves in the position of the people. Empathy invokes emotional intelligence competencies. For one to feel like the other person, he or she should first be aware of his or her emotional status. For instance, one has to understand how anger feels and how it manifests for him or her to understand how the other person is feeling. Empathy requires that we drop our personal biases and process the message and feedback from the other person in an open-minded manner. For instance, if listening to someone from a marginalized background one should not assume that they are ignorant and lazy. If we do not drop biases and stereotypes then it will be difficult to manifest empathy.

For example, if listening to an immigrant from Syria in the United States one should not assume that all they need is security and food. If you are interacting with such a person and you make assumptions that since the immigrant is from an Arab country then he or she is a Muslim then you are not being genuinely empathetic. Empathy requires letting the other person express their position and feelings and then taking place of the person to view the world through their lens. Perhaps a good illustration of empathy is how you felt when explaining yourself to a teacher why you came late but the teacher did not seem to share your position.

Body language

As indicated, body language is nonverbal communication and includes things like gestures, facial expressions, tone of voice, and posture among others. The biggest challenge with body language is that one has insignificant control as it largely initiated at the subconscious level of the brain. When you feel upset, you have little control over how you will react to the negative emotion. However, in this context, we are going to focus on how one can develop and employ nonverbal communication. The underpinning qualification of inclusion of nonverbal communication in communication skills is that they must align with verbal communication to make the message believable. Any contradiction between verbal and body language will portray one as acting or lying.

As such, one should try to ensure that they exhibit appropriate facial expressions and gestures when communicating. The most effective way to exhibit appropriate body language is to first internalize the message to enable evoke the appropriate emotion internally and externally. For instance, if the message of your communication bears happiness then one should first relate with the message before making a presentation. The other way of exhibiting appropriate body language is to make a mock presentation that can help you patch up on weak areas. As long as one has internalized the message then the matching emotions and body language will naturally manifest. The threats to manifesting appropriate body language include stage fright and cultural variations.

Clarity

It would surprise many that clarity of the message should occur in both verbal and nonverbal communication. Clarity of a message refers to the disambiguate-quality of communication making it easier for the masses to leave with one shared understanding. In the absence of clarity, each member of the audience will form their interpretation of the message. Poets and novelists frequently employ mild ambiguity in their work to interpret the message as open as possible. The clarity of a message should also include ensuring that the body language meaning is widely shared by the audience. However, in conventional communication clarity is a desired attribute when communicating.

For this reason, clarity includes the quality of not being ambiguous and using diction that many easily relate to. Clarity requires also ensuring that the communication flow is logical. The introductory part should precede the body of the message and the conclusion. One should use transition words such as firstly, previously, and for emphasis to enable the audience to follow. It is also necessary to give the audience moderate content rather than overloading the audience with information. Exhibiting clarity as a skill in communication requires that the speaker gathers and acts on feedback from the audience. Apart from feedback from the audience, self-feedback is useful as it enables the speaker to adjust communication accordingly.

Friendliness

Another one of the most overlooked skills in communication is friendliness. Friendliness is the quality of not being harsh. Even though friendliness is related to politeness, it is not synonymous with politeness. A friendly person is approachable even though the individual may not necessarily get along with you. A communicator should be friendly as judged by the tone of communication and body language. The audience should not feel judged or shouted at by the contents of the message or the speaker.

While we insist on exhibiting friendliness concerning the tone and content of the message in an exchange, it does not imply avoiding emotive issues. Friendliness may also include being considerate and sensitive to how others feel or react to a certain message. Friendliness will manifest with a genuine smile and measured gestures and facial expressions when invoking body language. The choice of words largely impacts on how the audience finds you friendly or hostile. There are cases where a speaker intended to sound friendly but his choice of words portrayed him on the contrary.

Respect

As part of communication skills, one should communicate in a manner that upholds and encourages respect. If people feel insulted or despised then this will make them switch off from active listening. Against this backdrop, a speaker should ensure that he is fully knowledgeable of the rich diversity of the audience. For instance, diversity includes attributes such as sex, gender, culture, ethnicity, socioeconomic status, and age. A man talking about an issue that affects women has to be considerate about how women view the issue. On the other hand, talking about the minority could be a sensitive issue especially where the main speaker is from the majority.

Relatedly, exhibiting respect in communication covers making appropriate and acceptable jokes and avoiding making jokes where one is unsure of the reaction of the audience. For instance, one should avoid making jokes about sexuality where intersex members exist in the audience. The gestures, facial expressions, and posture that a speaker exhibits may also communicate disdain or respect and the body language of the speaker should be respectful. When it comes to respecting, it is usually reciprocated which implies that showing respect to the audience through verbal communication and body language will motivate them to return the favor.

Coherence

In this context, coherence refers to the connectedness of the content and presentation. Even though one is free to start and interrupt a presentation, the content should be connected and with a clear flow of ideas. While speaking or pausing, a speaker should maintain the systematic development of the main idea of the message. Coherence requires that one stick to best practices when writing an essay such as having an introductory segment, building main points, and making a conclusion. One should make topical sentences and support them with evidence and examples. The use of transition words can help the audience make a connection between one segment of the presentation and the other.

In this manner, coherence is related to logic and rationality. When making a presentation avoid overloading the audience with information as this distorts the coherence of the presentation. The likelihood of weakness when it comes to coherence is likely to manifest when one pauses to make a light moment or allow questions from the audience. Questions from the audience should be related to the flow of the presentation to avoid making numerous diversionary comments.

Completeness

Notably, completeness as a skill concerns making communication that has an identifiable beginning and end and packed with the expected content. Using full sentences is one way of helping develop completeness in communication. One should provide all the relevant details when making communication. An example of completeness is when talks of gender and makes a distinction of gender and sex which helps make the audience full contextualize what is being defined. Completeness of information helps minimize questions and ambiguity. Expectedly, completeness as a skill in communication requires that one adequately prepare for the presentation.

Conciseness

The quality of being concise constitutes making the content of the message and coding as brief as possible without distorting the intended meaning. Conciseness does not mean summarizing information but presenting just what is needed. For this reason, conciseness leaves out verbosity as well as the use of jargon unless necessary. The aim of conciseness as the quality is to make the information easily understandable and memorable. Conciseness is highly desired for audiences with a language barrier and with older members. Itemizing the contents of the message as well as using transition phrases can help enhance the conciseness of a message.

Chapter 6: How to use empathy for better communication and influence other people

Empathy concerns placing oneself in the position of the other person and feeling how the other individual feels. As indicated, empathy requires that one first exhibit emotional awareness and emotional intelligence competencies. You can only understand the emotions are feeling if you first understand what those emotions are. Emotional intelligence deals with the capacity of an individual to understand and manage their own emotions including the ability to acknowledge and handle those of others. Some individuals inadvertently manage to relate with others immediately which allows them to feel special. It has been demonstrated that emotional intelligence is more useful than intellect and emotional intelligence can be improved well into later life through supportive coaching.

A humane speaker

Showing empathy can make one appear as listening and considerate. People find people that show care and concern highly relatable and real. If you exhibit empathy by showing an appropriate emotional reaction, body language and diction then the other individual will feel that he or she is being valued. If one does not feel valued then he or she is likely to abruptly end the conversation. A better illustration of this will require you to watch any episode of the TV series The Big Bang Theory and focus on Sheldon Palmer's character. One thing you will easily notice is that Sheldon Palmer's character appears insensitive to the feelings of others and this makes others feel misunderstood and undervalued which forces them to abruptly end the conversation. A person that exhibits empathy is likely to be relatable and believable to the target audience.

An influencer should use empathy to make the audience feel that he or she is humane and care for the audience's emotional needs. Through empathy, an influencer will manage to present himself as a friend of the target audience. Politicians understand the power of empathy and will always present themselves as caring and listening during the campaign period. While people have other needs, they prioritize the need to be understood and valued above others and this because it makes them feel that they are human beings and deserve dignity. Even though occasionally we need the bare facts and brutal truth, we largely value people that speak to us with care and concern.

Overcoming cultural barriers

In the contemporary world that is increasingly diverse, cultural barriers are inevitable. Cultural barriers negatively affect effective communication as well as the intended persuasion of the audience. Fortunately, a speaker can use body language and also read the body language of the other person to exhibit empathy. Empathy can help overcome cultural barriers, especially where one of the groups feels that the other does not comprehend how the minority one feels. Think of a Caucasian American showing appropriate emotions when talking about homicides in the African American community. Chances are that the target audience will find the speaker humane, relatable and understanding.

Cultural barriers manifest when the message and the coding, whether verbally or nonverbally, varies significantly across different ethnicities. In this context, cultural barriers include religious affiliations. The cultural barriers are likely to be compounded with diction, which can make the audience feel disenfranchised. Fortunately, empathy allows the speaker to invoke body language to show appropriate emotions and bridge this cultural barrier. The audience is likely to understand the efforts of the speaker and process the message as envisioned by the speaker. When attempting to influence in the context of cultural barriers one should focus more on the tone of voice, facial expressions, gestures, and postures to compensate for the gap in relating to the audience verbally.

Overcoming language barriers

Relatedly to cultural barriers, language barriers will affect effective communication and ultimately degrade persuasion. Language barriers include the inability of two people to decode the message verbally, and decreased ability to understand the message due to the language used to code the message. There are some contexts where the language barrier is unavoidable especially in multicultural social events. In these settings, people may be non-fluent speakers of a particular language and will struggle to grasp the intended meaning. A speaker that relies entirely on verbal communication will not manage to communicate and influence the audience.

As indicated, the speaker can salvage the situation by exhibiting empathy. The speaker should use the appropriate tone of voice when communicating to help all the members of the audience relate.

Overcoming emotional barriers

Emotions affect the way we process a message as well as the way we react to a message. Emotions are largely a learned function in that we manifest particular emotions depending on our past experiences and expectations. For instance, through past experiences, we learned that attaining high scores signals more opportunities and for this reason, we will show positive emotions when we manage to get on the list. On the contrary, we will show frustrations when fail to score the highest or expected scores. Emotions are complex in that we rarely have control of how and when they manifest. When attempting to influence, your emotions and those of the target will affect the effectiveness of the message.

Fortunately, through empathy, we can make it easier to defuse emotional reactions. For instance, by showing that you share the emotions of the other person the individual may quickly and safely process the emotions. Think of an individual that is angry but you show that you understand why he or she is feeling this way. Chances are that the individual is likely to quickly defuse the intense emotions and unblock the mind for listening. Through empathy, we avoid judging the person as emotional or unstable. A good influencer will exploit an emotional moment to project himself or herself as considerate and patient, which will win the person. The other advantage of accommodating the emotions of the other person is that the individual propagates the communication to others expanding the scope of influence.

Aligning verbal and nonverbal communication

Often, verbal and nonverbal communication contradicts each other, which distorts the message. The contradiction between verbal communication occurs when oral communication does not align with the body language of the individual. For instance, if you say you are feeling peaceful but your facial expressions and posture suggest panic and uneasiness then you will appear like you are being dishonest. Any contradiction between verbal communication and nonverbal communication will make one less believable when interacting with the target audience. There are several ways to correct the contradiction between verbal communication and body language and one of them is exhibiting empathy.

Against this backdrop, empathizing with the audience can make them harmonize the gap between verbal communication and body language. As indicated, empathy requires that takes the position of the other person and processes their feelings. Through learning to exhibit genuine emotions one will likely exhibit matching body language which will enhance verbal and nonverbal communication. Assume that you are talking about ethnic profiling and you take time to feel like a victim of the vice. Chances are that you are likely to exhibit appropriate facial expressions, postures, and tone of voice, which will make it easier for effective communication and set the stage of convincing the target audience.

Enhanced timing when communicating

Communication relies on appropriate timing. While communication is continuous concerning body language, verbal communication depends on timing. For instance, you will pause or take a break if the feedback from the audience indicates that the audience is feeling tired. The reason you are stopping or taking a break is that you have empathized with the audience. Empathizing with the audience implied that you share how they feel and are considering their physiological and emotional needs. For this reason, empathy contributes significantly to timing in communication. Without timing, making communication effective especially verbal communication would be difficult.

In other terms, empathy enables the communicator to understand when to take a break, when to unleash information, and when to allow the audience to participate. All these are possible because empathy requires that the speaker occasionally takes the viewpoint of the audience. For this reason, the speaker genuinely understands the exhaustion and emotions of the audience. Concerning influencing, empathy improves the timing of delivery of communication and eventually influence. Overall, empathy makes the speaker relatable and is perceived as caring.

Chapter 7: Tips to help people become a better friend, a better parent, a better partner, better businessman or women, outlining the beliefs or mental habits that one person should cultivate to use successful negotiation methods in daily life situations.

Becoming a partner person requires exhibiting certain attributes that we shall underline.

Becoming a better friend

In this context, a friend is a person that one can relate and feels comfortable opening up even when the individual is not related to you by blood. Becoming a great friend requires that one acts in a considerate manner. For this reason, one should empathize with others by feeling the way they feel. Your colleagues will find you a listening and understandable person if you share how they feel. For instance, you will understand why a friend acts in the manner he does if you share their emotions. An example is a colleague who seems absent-minded because she has received a retrenchment letter. If you react by showing mild shock and hugging the colleague, it will portray you as a caring person.

Relatedly, you should be involved in the life of your friend to make him or her feel that you value him or her. Each one of us wants to feel valued and especially if it is a friend making us feel treasured. The other way of making someone feel valued is to ask them how they are feeling. We often ignore probing the status and welfare of our colleagues because we assume if they are smiling, they are okay. However, our friends do appreciate it when we go out of our way to prove their status. It shows that we are involved in and care about their welfare. Being regarded as caring indicates that one is shelving their interests to accommodate others.

As such, a good friend must first understand their emotions. Drawing from emotional intelligent competencies, one should be self-aware of their feelings. Without understanding your emotions, you will have difficulties safely projecting those emotions and enabling your colleagues to read them. The mistake most people make is to assume that they are the only ones that should exhibit considerations. It is important to assert oneself and enable the other person to understand your feelings and beliefs. If you do not make your feelings known then you will feel used by your friends. A good friend makes his status known to enable others to adjust.

Becoming a better parent

Parenting involves a lot but for this context, parenting entails providing emotional, economical, personal and spiritual needs to a child until the child shows partial to full independence. Predictably, the role of parenting is wide and this elicits challenges of exhaustion, frustration, and uncertainty. Even for the most prepared parent, parenting is a challenge as each child shows unique character and personality that may take time to read and manage. In most cases parents especially new parents have to rely on varying views from friends and online searches regarding parenting. We are going to offer tips on how to enhance parenting.

Firstly, a parent should be seen as listening. For this reason, when a parent demonstrates that he or she is listening by nodding, eye contact and reflecting than the child will feel that the parent is interested in their lives. Children like any human being want to feel that someone is listening to what they are trying to say. Children require more patience and accommodation when handling them and failure to listen to them will affect them psychologically. If a child feels that the parent is a listening kind then he or she is likely to open up and confide in the parent.

Secondly, a parent should read and act on feedback provided by the child. Children give feedback either verbally or nonverbally. For instance, a child that maintains distance when speaking is likely to be feeling uncomfortable and the parent should understand this. Reading and acting on verbal and nonverbal feedback will enhance not only communication but also the value of communication. Since children are still at various developmental stages, a parent must learn to read and act on feedback provided by a parent. A parent that reads the feedback given is likely to be perceived as responsive and loving.

Becoming a better partner

Relationships require social skills and exhibiting social skills requires emotional intelligence competencies. One way of becoming a better partner is to read the body language of the other person. For instance, if your partner sits far away from you than usual then he or she is communicating that he no longer feels safe. Sitting physically far off from you than usual communicates that he or she may also be feeling temperamental and does not trust that the emotions will dissipate safely. Think of a situation where you are visibly angry and almost shaking but the other person fails to read this emotion.

Relatedly, one should be accommodative of the other partner. Accepting the preferences and weaknesses of the other partner is central to forming a lasting relationship. There is a lot of diversity within a relationship and this includes sex, gender, religion, ethnicity, and socioeconomic status. This diversity implies that partners are sensitive to certain words, remarks, gestures, and dressing. While the affected partner may seem at ease with a flattery remark regarding their sex, gender, ethnicity, and religion they might be highly offended. In relationships, one can play along with unease topics for long but they will snap at some point.

Additionally, being a good partner requires that one empathizes with how the other person feels. A common shortcoming in a relationship is that the partner's mistake empathizing with carrying the burden of the other person. If one of the partners is angry because he lost money, it should not mean that you stop everything scheduled to attend to the emotions of the other partner. It is for this reason that some people think that listening to people is burdensome since they tend to carry the burden of the other person. However, listening to a partner simply means empathizing with them, acting sensitively, and not shouldering the burdens of your partner.

Becoming a better business person

Business involves frequent human interaction, which is the main reason for organizations investing in customer relationship management. A business has to exhibit a human face which includes engaging in numerous corporate social responsibility programs. The public expects a lot from businesses and indeed business persons. Against this backdrop, a business person is expected to be formal, friendly, and creative. In this discussion, we will focus on aspects of being formal, creative and friendly. Unlike the general population, a business person is judged as well as his or her business. In some cases, people do not distinguish between the public and private life of a businessperson, which can make the life of a businessperson highly rehearsed and unfulfilling.

Firstly, a businessperson should be friendly to endear oneself to others and especially the customers. Using the appropriate diction and tone will help cultivate an image of a professional and friendly business and businessperson. For this reason, a businessperson should speak with a firm and calm voice to create a perception of reassurance and confidence. Diction concerns the choice of words and diction does not imply using jargon. Instead, diction concerns selecting and using words that elicit the intended meaning as well as the right emotion when addressing the audience. Think of addressing the public during a crisis, using the right words is critical for one to sound believable.

Secondly, a businessperson should show concern when dealing with others. A person should create the impression that he or she is listening. In business, customers are bound to make complaints and offer suggestions. Customers should not feel judged or intimidated or dismissed by body language and verbal communication when communicating with the public. For instance, if you listen to customer complaints without noting them down or nodding then the customer will feel that he or she is inconsequential to the business. Showing concern includes making a follow-up and personally contacting the customer when remedial measures are taken. Showing concern includes respecting the order of customer demands and acting on them accordingly.

Thirdly, a businessperson should have fidelity to his words and promises. Consistency is highly desired if one is a businessperson. For this reason, a businessperson should understand that each talk he or she has is seen as an official statement inseparable from personal and official duties. While a businessperson may want to avoid taking hard stances, showing consistency is important and for that reason, a businessperson should take a neutral position. Assuming a neutral position will enable a person to safely accommodate the diversity of his customers. However, they are instances where a business person has to take a clear stance and these include issues regarding the environment, human life, and position of customers in the business model of the company. The position taken has to be consistent.

Mental habits of a successful negotiator

An astute negotiator takes time to perform a quick background analysis of the impasse. One cannot just start negotiating without understanding the context of the negotiation and the viewpoint taken by the feuding members. Where possible, one should determine the economic, philosophical, social and power status of the feuding partners before initiating a conversation on the standoff. Parties in a negotiation tend to invoke their philosophical, power, and social principles as well as the power distance when maintaining their hardline position. Once a skilled negotiator familiarizes with all these developments then he or she is set to initiate a meaningful conversation.

An astute negotiator needs to take charge of the process. In an impasse, each party would want to dominate the conversation, which enables them to crowd out the alternating views of the other party. A good negotiator will ensure fairness and discipline during a negotiation, which is necessary to make each party feel respected and valued. Sometimes due to intense emotions, a party in a negotiation will seek to stop further proceeding by exploiting any phrases that appear disrespectful and seek to halt and propagate the standoff. Feuding parties will use any minor indiscipline issues to validate their hard stance. A seasoned negotiator will always emphasize on the core issues that necessitated the negotiation.

As such, a good negotiator is patient. Situations that necessitate negotiation often invoke intense emotions that may touch on race, economic status, sex, gender, religion, and workload. Such issues can make it difficult to make any meaningful discussions. In most cases, a section of the feuding parties would want the standoff to continue as it brings about free time, relaxed rules, relaxed supervision and a temporarily improved power distance for the affected. For this reason, most feuding parties would not want an immediate solution even though they still need one. A seasoned negotiator should understand this and patiently navigate the standoff by achieving any little progress such as the feuding parties meeting and shaking hands.

Most importantly, a good negotiator is neutral. If one is not careful, he or she will take positions that can significantly compromise the negotiation. Individually we have our political stand, philosophical views, religious affiliations, subscribing to a certain school of ethics, and have different beliefs of a progressive society. Without having comprehensive self-feedback and personal values, it is easy to be sucked into the feud and favor one side unknowingly. A great negotiator simply guides the conversation between the feuding parties and maintains neutrality.

Chapter 8: Influence in dating and relationships

Given chance, most people would want to exert influence in relationships but do not expertise. As earlier indicated, relationships require social skills which in turn depend significantly on emotional intelligence competencies. For emphasis, one has to first become aware of their emotions and learn to safely manifest these emotions to make it easier for others to react accordingly. If one cannot express all of their emotions then it will become difficult for others to correctly read and adjust to the status of the person. The next step is for the person to exhibit social skills such as empathy, and exerting one position during social interactions.

Against this backdrop, social skills will include the ability to persuade and impact skills in others. Communication skills and conflict management skills are part of the ways of influencing people in a relationship. If one possesses social skills concerning emotional intelligence then you will also possess leadership skills. Change management skills are integral to social skills and building rapport is another social skill applied in emotional intelligence. One should also possess collaboration and cooperation competencies to become socially skilled to increase influence in a relationship.

Firstly, improve your persuasion skills by recognizing the strengths of the other person. We all have weaknesses but we do not like being reminded about the need to improve. We tend to appreciate a person that recognizes and emphasizes our strengths. For this reason, you should recognize and underscore the positives about an individual, which does not mean overlooking the weaknesses of the person. In a relationship, most people seek acceptance and civility including care. By highlighting, the best that a person presents we will make the individual feel honored and celebrated which makes it easier to impact him or her.

Secondly, one should communicate by exhibiting astute communication skills. Learn to listen to the other person and focus your thoughts and your feelings. Make the individual understand what is you are trying to communicate by giving complete and accurate information. Part of communication skills will require that you become prepared to learn about challenges and not just wanting to receive good news. If you are a good influencer, you will handle challenging issues directly as opposed to letting problems build up. Ensure that the message that you are packaging is appropriate and act on resultant emotional cues.

Equally important, one needs to possess and apply conflict management skills in a relationship. Conflicts are inevitable in relationships and without threshold conflict resolution skills the relationship is bound to be uncertain and burdensome. For this reason, conflicts are unavoidable and sometimes not predictable. Both at home and at work, the art of managing and resolving conflict is critical. Conflict management skills start with becoming aware of the critical tact and diplomacy and how these competencies can be applied to defuse emotive situations. A good influencer will confront disagreements and help resolve them. Most important is that conflict resolution does not involve you imposing the solution rather helping the affected parties identify the different opinions, the fears and shared understanding to craft a solution. When resolving conflicts, we should emphasize more on the logical position to create a shared understanding among the conflicting parties.

Relatedly, one needs to demonstrate leadership skills to attain effective persuasion in a relationship. In most relationships, there is a need to show the other partner the way forward and this calls for deploying leadership skills. The ability to influence requires that you align your emotions and those of others to win them over. Influence is a critical attribute of good leadership. It is often called charisma but though leadership skills involving influence go beyond charisma to match good emotional intelligence. The competencies of good leadership require you to articulate a vision to enable others to follow it. Closely related to demonstrated to leadership is the need for one to be accountable.

Expectedly, the relationship has to change and it is natural for the other partner to resist due to fear of uncertainty. A good influencer has to exhibit change management skills. Change catalysts can be effective influencers and individuals that make a change to materialize while involving everyone are widely admired. For all people concerned, change tends to create pressure partly because of the fear of the unknown. As such, good change management skills require one to make it an interesting opportunity rather than a threat. Change catalysts acknowledge the criticality of change and eliminate barriers. The resistance to change is because it disrupts the status quo and advocates for change. Leading by example is a common attribute of change catalysts to trigger desired adjustments.

Consequently, one should build rapport. It is important to create and maintain constructive relationships with other persons. Mastering this skill will help create improved relationships and enhance the ability to work and succeed in life. Persons that are good with building bonds are great networkers, create and maintain a robust network of connections and contacts. Building a rapport involves establishing relationships to maintain it healthy. If you exhibit good rapport as a competence then you are likely to have many friends. The essence of building bonds is to value others and being interested in their lives as well as being eager to learn more about them.

In a relationship, we have to work as a team to build a shared future. Individuals with good collaboration skills will build good and productive working including relationships and some people function well with others. All these attributes are important when building social skills in emotional intelligence. People with collaborative skills will see relationships as critical as the pending task and will value people as much as they consider the activity at hand. If you have collaboration skill then you will actively cooperate, share ideas and plans, and work with others to create an improved whole. In this ideal environment, the other partner will feel inspired to contribute to the building of the joint future. If you possess the collaboration and cooperative competence then you will actively lookout for opportunities for cooperative working.

For emphasis, creating meaningful relationships with your partner can significantly lower tension and apprehension in your life. Enhancing your social support is associated with improved mental health as having reliable friends can serve as a safety net for low mood and anxiety. For some people, anxiety pushes them to avoid social situations and holds them from building relationships. If one is socially anxious and desperately wants to create friends but is reluctant then he or she is likely to seclude himself from social situations. One of the outcomes of social seclusion is that one will miss out on building upon their confidence in interacting with others. Start by creating robust communication skills that would enhance the likelihood of successful relationships.

As suggested, the pillar to cultivating and maintain friendships is communication skills. These skills are critical when developing a strong social support network. Having communication skills will enable you to take care of your individual needs while remaining respectful of the needs of your partner. Persons are not born with good communication skills like all the other skills. We learn communication skills through trial and error as well as a consistent practice. The three significant areas for communication are assertiveness, conversation skills, and non-verbal communication. Communication has several aspects besides the one stated above such as presentation skills, managing conflict and giving feedback.

One of the often-overlooked areas in relationships is the importance and meaning of body language. Nonverbal communication constitutes a large part of what we communicate. In practice, what your body language speaks is more powerful than what you verbalize. If you feel anxious you will act in ways that are intended to avoid communicating with others. An example is when you avoid eye contact or speak softly. In this instance, you are trying not to communicate and possibly avoid being judged adversely by your partner. Nevertheless, the tone of voice and body language communicate effective messages about your emotional state, the attitude displayed towards the listener and comprehension of the topic. If you are avoiding eye contact and standing far from others as well as speaking within a muffled voice then you are communicating that that you are not feeling comfortable. There are chances that this was not your intentioned message.

An equally important aspect of the relationship and that is related to exerting influence is being assertive. About the communication, assertive communication concerns an honest expression of your individual needs, feelings and wants while respecting those of the other person. If you are an assertive communicator then your mien is non-threatening and non-judgmental as well as you take accountability for your actions.
For instance, if you feel anxious you will experience some difficulty in sharing your thoughts and feelings. Even though assertiveness can be a challenge to master as being assertive can hold you back from the way you operate, it can be acquired with commitment. An illustration is when you are afraid of conflict and chose to tag along with the opinion of the masses instead of giving your opinions. In this sense, you are becoming a passive communicator. You may target to manage and dominate others and this is a sign of aggressive communication style. Fortunately, the assertive communication approach has many benefits. Assertive communication can help you relate to others more genuinely and lessen hopelessness.

There are several misconceptions about being assertive such as being assertive implies having your way each time. One of the myths about assertiveness is that it implies loading your opinions on others but this is not true. If you are assertive, it means that you are voicing your position and communicating honestly with others. In some instances, you might win your way by assertively voicing your opinion. Informing others how you feel and attempting to reach a compromise is an indication that you respect yourself and others.

Relatedly, some wrongly believe that being assertive implies being selfish. A misconception is that assertiveness creates selfishness. However, being assertive does not imply that you are being inconsiderate or uncaring to your partner. Assertiveness is not aggressiveness as asserting your position will still leave room for others to agree or disagree with your views.

Equally, important people in a relationship wrongly assume that being passive will make them loveable. A false belief is that you can only be loved when you are passive. It is counterproductive to be passive as it suggests that one is always agreeing with other persons and always allowing them to have their way. Passivity involves giving in to the wishes of others and making no demands of your own. Being passive does not guarantee that you will be admired by other persons. If you are passive, other people might consider you dull and disinterested in what they are transacting.

In the same breath, some people wrongly assume that is rude to disagree. It is a false assumption is that it is impolite to disagree. Even though there are instances where we might not be honest, in most cases people are interested in what we truly think about them. Imagine how you would feel if each person always agreed with you. Chances are that you would find such people dishonest and shallow.

In relationships, one can enhance their value and admiration by exercising calm during social strife moments. When feeling anxious, your brain will cease working effectively irrespective of the many social skills that you possess. If one is upset then it becomes a challenge to sustain coherence and logic of the conversation. Learning to calm down is important as well as relaxing in social situations helps in another excessively. Due to the nonverbal cue, aspect of communication, your body and face can portray you as nervous and this will create difficulty for others to feel at ease when trying to strike a rapport with you, speaking well is not the only aspect of good social skills.

Correspondingly, a relationship can be improved by enhancing active listening as an art. Partners feel good when someone listens to them. Proper listening skills mean that you actively acknowledge listening such as nodding the head, taking notes, sustaining eye contact and making acknowledgment noises. Providing feedback through nonverbal and verbal reaction is part of ideal listenership. You should also refer back to comments of others later on such letting them know you needed more clarification with earlier statements. It is also important to maintain physical alertness and attentiveness while the other person is speaking. One should learn to develop an interest in others to enable you to develop an interest in what they presenting.

Repeatedly, one should focus on ways of building rapport in a relationship. The state of understanding in a good social interaction is known as rapport. Creating a rapport implies that you make the person understand that you are indifferent to him or her and it occurs at the subconscious level of the mind. Creating a rapport involves seeking to establish a pattern and rhythm that harnesses the different speech patterns, speech rhythms, diction and personalities to create synergy. Rapport concerns a state of connection that happens in a good social interaction. Striking rapport implies that you are like the other person and that you understand each other. Social skills training can enhance rapport such as body posture reflection. When interacting with someone align your expressions and body posture. You should not mimic, as this should happen at the unconscious level. Feeding back what you have listened to is also important. A rapport is that which makes you feel connected to someone you did not share your childhood with and it is effortless.

If one wants to become an influencer, he or she must understand the extent that he or she talks about oneself. When interacting with another person avoid talking about your life, so much as this can be irritating to the other person. It is suggested that you start with small talk on non-personal issues or sharing of personal views in a balanced way. In instances, when you describe your greatest desires and major fears to a new acquaintance you will freak them out. As the relationship and conversations progress you can disclose personal facts starting with small and non-emotional ones first. When progressively disclosing personal facts it will lead to a feeling of wanting to know each other.

Chapter 9: Influence of friendship

Even though related to the previous chapter, exerting influence in a relationship differs slightly with impacting a relationship. As human beings, we are inclined to exert influence in friendships and learning about explicit and subtle ways can help one accomplish this. Situations where we want to exert influence including when we want our friends to subscribe to our beliefs or arguments without giving them ultimatums. Sometimes we might want to exert influence over trivial issues such as getting our friends to support our team.

Firstly, learn about the preferences and dislikes of your friend. First understanding what our friends' values and dislikes are important. Even though this seems like a cliché, few people invest time in understanding their friends. For instance, dig deeper to find out if your friend has health issues, family issues, work issues, mental health issues as well as their favorite snack and movie. Showing interest and understanding of what your friends want helps make them feel valued and are likely to be more receptive to your message. For this reason, showing a keen interest in the life of your friend will motivate the person to allow more views and suggestions from you.

Secondly, show concern about the feelings and worries of your friend. An often-overlooked aspect of friendship is acknowledging and respecting the emotions of our friends. In most cases, we hurriedly urge our friends to cheer up instead of first empathizing with our friends. Lack of recognizing and relating to the emotions expressed by our friends makes them more empty and is likely to make them hide their emotions rather than express them. An individual that encourages their friends to show emotions is likely to come across as a humane and relatable person, which will make the individual more receptive to message, and suggestions from the concerned.

Thirdly, take note of the nonverbal cues of your friend. As indicated, body language is a critical and continuous form of communication unless verbal communication. Additionally, body language can provide a hint of the emotional status of the individual and this should make reading and act on the body language of the friend critical. For instance, if your friend sits in a slumped position and stares at the ceiling there is a chance that the friend is exhausted or distracted even when the individual insists that she is okay. It is natural for human beings to take time before sharing negative feelings due to self-preservation.

Fourthly, notice the changes in your friend and adjust accordingly. Human behavior is dynamic and the environment is gradually changing. Human beings have to adjust accordingly to enhance their survivability. We are changing and so are our friends. Unfortunately, we rarely take the cue that there are changes in the life of our friends save for major changes such as childbirth, marriage, and employment and health issues. Some of the issues we regard as trivial affect the emotional status of our friends and this includes having a nagging partner, job transfer, new work rules, and change of service providers by our friends. Even though these developments appear trivial, they significantly disturb the established pattern of living by our friends and should be explored.

Fifthly, make your feelings and your limits are known. As argued earlier, a common mistake that we make is to ignore our welfare at the expense of our friends. Some people wrongly assume that exerting one's feelings and views imply being selfish and inconsiderate to our friends. In reality, making your views known enables others to understand your limits and respect your attempts. If one does not define their limits there is a risk of the person feeling used and exhausted by the friendship. Lack of exerting one's views in the early days of friendship is among the leading causes of dropping friends or giving up on acquiring friends altogether.

Sixthly, learn to moderate your availability in the friendship. Having a working friendship does not imply foregoing everything including your time to sustain friendships. It is important to understand that there are three circles of friendship and these include the close-knit circle, strategic friends circle, and public-space friends circle. The close-knit friends are those acquaintances that we have allowed in almost every aspect of our lives and are akin to a family. The strategic friends' circle includes those acquaintances we intend to benefit from them while they also expect to gain from us and these include classmates, neighbors, and workmates. Lastly, the public-space circles of friends are largely networking friends where the interaction is largely formal and on a need-be basis.

Equally important you should be accommodative to your friend. The contemporary world is global and diverse. Chances are that your friends come from diverse ethnicities, religious affiliation, different sexes, and different economic classes. The modern world often sets up to having and meeting diverse people, which calls for being open-minded and sensitive to how others feel. Even though your friends might be at ease with flattery remarks about their sex, race and economic class, one should seek to minimize the need to explicitly invoke defining demographics for diversity. With time, your friends may feel judged and simply back off rather than confront you on the issue. A person that is open-minded and accommodative of others is highly respected and valued by others.

Chapter 10: Influence in parenting

As earlier on discussed, parenting covers a lengthy period and involves multiple spheres in the life of a child. Parents face challenges to successfully fulfill their caregiver role concerning the cultural, economic, nutritional, educational, health, and psychological needs of a child. Against this backdrop, a parent needs skills and information on how to influence the child to the preferred direction in life. The following presentations will help a parent exert influence over their children.

Firstly, show respect and concern to the child. Start by listening and responding to the concerns of your child. Even though this appears a cliché, most parents do not find it critical to always listen and act on the wishes of their children. Acting on the wishes of your child does not mean procuring everything that your child demands but it implies acknowledging that you are aware of the requests and giving feedback. Amazingly, most children understand even though they may require sustained repetition. Disrespecting a child includes rudely shutting the demands of the child or rudely reminding the child about your life challenges. Building a lasting relationship with your child starts with minding their welfare, which does not imply giving them everything they request.

Secondly, allow criticism and negative feedback from the child. Related to the first argument, most parents loathe receiving criticism from their children. Most parents take criticism from their children as stating they are poor parents and proceed to shut their children by shouting at the children. Criticism from your child is just that, criticism. When you allow respectful criticism from your child, it enables the child to become freer with you and listens more. By allowing criticism from your child, you are making yourself a partner and friend of the child, which enhances the bond between the parent and the child.

Thirdly, focus more on your body language and that of the child. While most parents acknowledge the importance of body language, they tend to discourage it or overlook it as their children grow. Most parents will often urge their children to speak up which is an implication that they want their children to verbalize. However, children should be allowed to use body language, as it accurately communicates not just their feelings but emotional status as well. It is common for children to freeze their words when they notice another person in the presence of their parents when coming to report an issue. Focusing on body language will allow a parent to have an additional source of feedback apart from verbalized feedback and act on it accordingly.

Fourthly, where possible as a parent lead by example. For children, demonstrating what you want goes a long way into persuading them that it is possible. Unlike adults, most children may not manage to read or search for information on their account and for this reason, it is necessary to show them a demonstration. For example, if you want your children to watch television less start by watching with them and then stating that let us go out and play table tennis. Using this example, as a parent you have demonstrated and next time you issue instructions for them to cut down on watching television and play outdoor they are likely to follow your instructions without whining.

Fifthly, use games and activities to emphasize your message and values. Children have relatively short concentration spans and prefer fun activities. For instance, rather than lecture, your children on good grades or hygiene take time to play with them. After playing with your children when taking a break, give them advice on the importance of working hard and maintaining good body hygiene. Chances are that the children are likely to remember what they were told when doing fun activities. However, emphasis should be made that these activities have to be outdoor activities such as kicking a ball, tying strings on structures or sliding. The justification for such activities is that they offer physical and mental stimulation that makes it easier to enjoy and remember.

Equally important, manage the exposure of information to the child to help influence the desired outcome. Like with any form of influence, being in control of the flow and quality of information is critical to exerting influence on your children. It is necessary that you carefully monitor and filter information are given to your children. Concerning information, information is the clay that we mold with our flower vase. Like molding a flower vase, it is best done when it is gradual and allowing the mold to dry before baking it to hardness and that is true to exposure of children to information. Children are exposed to information via television programs, phone applications, and the Internet and computer games. A parent that wants to maintain influence should seek to filter these sites of exposure to information to their children to ensure that information accessed by the children is consistent with the parenting deployed.

Chapter 11: Influence at workplace

Apart from relationships, the other place where influence is highly desired is at the workplace. At the workplace, one may seek to exert influence as a team leader, supervisor or colleague. A workmate may seek to exert influence in readiness for one day seeking a leadership position at the organization. Like different spheres of life, most people assume that they have the competencies to influence when in reality they are not. Contemporary workplaces are diverse in terms of religion, ethnicity, sex, gender and socioeconomic status. All of us have some degree of bias because we were raised by parents and society that subtly imparted in us.

Start by showing interest in the views of your colleagues. Almost everyone wants to be where he or she is valued. One way of showing that you treasure a colleague is to salute them, ask about their status and wish them a great day. While all these appear known, most people still struggle to express interest in the lives of their colleagues. The second way of expressing interest in the life of your colleagues is to read their body language and adjust your approach and communication. The other way of demonstrating an interest in the lives of your colleagues is making suggestions about new places and products that align with their interests. All these developments help make the target person feel wanted and treasured.

Sometimes all one needs to do is spend more time with colleagues to exert influence over them. Most people may not be spending adequate time with friends to establish a rapport and make them understand you. Spending time with friends can help them adequately profile you and appreciate your views. For some people, spending time with friends is akin to idling. For others spending time with friends does not deliver, as most of them are embroiled on social media applications and other distractions. Try to reflect the minutes or hours that you spend with colleagues, most likely you will discover that is far shorter which limits your impact.

Relatedly show accommodativeness. As suggested, modern workplaces manifest rich diversity in terms of sex, ethnicity, economic status, and religious affiliations. The contemporary workplaces are teaming up with women and men that must work together to accomplish given tasks. The continuous close contact requires that both sexes communicate courteously. For ethnicity, and subtle to the explicit form of discrimination based on race and tribe will be emotive and can have legal repercussions. The same is true for people in your team from varying economic class and religious affiliations. Unlearning and moderation are critical in navigating these sensitive issues.

Additionally, apply emotional intelligence to endear yourself to others. Through emotional intelligence, one learns to understand their emotions and express them safely. The overriding emphasis of emotional intelligence is that each emotion including negative emotions should be safely expressed. Think of a leader that when upset shakes and bangs tables. While such a person may be charismatic, few people will find the person safe to approach especially when presenting emotive issues. Emotional intelligence competencies emphasize understanding self and in particular the emotions. Through emotional intelligence, we learn how to anticipate and manage our extreme emotions.

Relatedly, exert your position and limits. When interacting with other people one should take the earliest opportunity to define their limits. Lack of defining limits will imply that one feels exhausted and used. Think of being uncomfortable making a speech but since you did not explicitly make your members aware of this preference, you are left to grudgingly shoulder this task. Most people often feel used and exploited in-group activities because of a lack of exerting their positions. A common myth is that exerting your position will deny your friends and that it makes you be perceived as a self-centered individual. However, the benefits of defining your limits are that you will get a friend circle that closely aligns with your preferences.

Correspondingly, show cultural competence. Showing cultural competence is closely linked to diversity issues in the workplace. Apart from just being accommodative at the workplace, one should aspire to have a basic understanding of known cultures to enhance empathy and respect. Think of an individual having a team member from the Japanese culture where handshakes are not preferred and the person is working in corporate America. Without the basic understanding of the Japanese culture, one will keep on pestering the affected person to embrace handshakes at the workplace. For this reason, cultural competence goes further to require that one reads or watches basic aspects of the target culture to enable him or her to value diversity at the workplace.

Equally, importance, learn to demonstrate honesty. At the workplace, workplace politics exist and they tend to create two major opposing sides though the differences are mild and highly navigable. On any issue, employees tend to subscribe to two sides, which is acceptable. Issues start when one or several employees fail to demonstrate honesty by switching sides, which can make others distrust the particular colleague as a snitch, saboteur or dishonest individual. It is at this stage that conflicts start to simmer. Against this backdrop, one should strive to be honest and consistent to make it easier for other workers to appreciate the position taken. For emphasis, taking opposing sides is not an issue but lack of consistency and honesty is.

Against this backdrop, one should await an invitation to join a conversation. Showing respect to your colleagues includes understanding when to join a conversation. Just because your colleagues are talking does not necessarily qualify you to join the conversation. One should always pick cues from others to know when to join or leave a conversation. For instance, if your friends are talking and they are rarely looking at you or mentioning your name then the cue here is that you should give them space to conclude their conversation. Similarly, one should take cues of when to leave a conversation. In cases where one is a conversation, the other parties may want him or her to exit the conversation and he or she should take cues.

Lastly, focus more on the strengths than weaknesses of your colleagues. Your workmates have shortcomings and may not want to be reminded of what they lack. Pointing out the weaknesses of your colleague amounts to profiling him or her, which is a development that many loathe. Even though it seems an easy thing, it is not always possible to avoid mentioning or implying shortcomings. With practice, one can learn to gradually focus more on the strengths of an individual. Focusing on strengths requires remaining in the moment and avoiding biases. With biases, we are bound to have a predetermined projection of a person, which can make us focus on their shortcomings than their strengths.

An illustration of a situation at the workplace concerns Davis who wants to persuade members at his workplace to form a support group to enable them to handle minor mental health issues including relationship challenges. The reason for wanting to create an informal support group stems from the fact that most workers' domestic life impacts their formal life and vice versa. Since most of the domestic issues relating to the time spent at work including associated exhaustion, most workers agree that the workplace is the best place to confront the issue. A quick scan of issues suggests that workload, diversity issues, and performance appraisal have enhanced the risk for mental health issues at the workplace. Most people fail to leave work life effects at the workplace and bring them home.

Correspondingly, Davis can enhance his influence at the workplace by knowing members through greeting them and asking them how their day is so far. By saluting the workers, Davis will make them feel recognized and cared for. With the workers feeling valued, Davis can challenge them to do something about their plight, which is a negative effect of workplace challenges on their personal lives. Having established a shared position with the majority of the members, Davis can then invoke body language to attain appropriate timing to make the members feel that it is time to act. Using cultural competence Davis can safely navigate the sensitive issues in the audience by being open-minded, empathetic and patient with each member contributing.

Predictably, the colleagues of Davis are likely to feel that he is visionary and considerate. Davis is likely to use the group dynamics by selectively winning over a few people who will, in turn, convert more. Where possible, Davis is likely to exploit the diversity among the members to buy into his ideas. Additionally, Davis is likely to invoke authority and logic to win over more members. Appealing to authority may include quoting renowned psychologists on workplace stress and its effect on personal relationships. Making the workmates see the reasonability of having a support group can help persuade them further. People value figures of authority and this requires invoking authority.

Overall, influencing people does not necessarily imply standing before them and asking them to carry out something. Influencing people can happen when one is just a member of a team. For instance, you need to show empathy and consideration to others for them to find you believable. Maintaining consistency is important when seeking to persuade people. People want to follow someone who they can trust will maintain the tempo even when cornered by authorities. Exhibiting requisite communication competencies is important, as communication is critical in coding the message to the target audience. Think of people or friends with great ideas but struggle to communicate these ideas to the target audiences. Such people are likely not having any impact on their target audiences.

Chapter 12: Influence in advertising

Influence in advertising is a central purpose of carrying advertisements in the first place. Organizations run adverts to enhance their visibility and draw more people to their product offers. Unlike any other application of influence, advertising depends significantly on convincing the masses. Adverts also act as reminders and predictive programming that subtly draws the customer to the advertised product. When making an advert we focus on its features that the consumer will enjoy. In this chapter, we are going to present different ways to enhance influence in advertising.

Firstly, employ repetition. In advertising, the potency is in repetition. The advert and the message should be repeated to make it be treated as a fact. A message repeated several times is often treated as truth. At one point, you must have believed that Coca Cola's Coke is the symbol of refreshing taste because the advert has been repeated several times. A marketing message rendered via several media and repeated several times is eventually treated as a fact. It is for this reason that companies invest significantly to deliver a brief message that is repeated on all mainstream and social media channels.

Another illustration of the power of repetition is the Gillette Blue advert, which repeats that the shaver is the best that a man can get. There are chances that better shavers exist but the sustained repetition has emphasized the features of Gillette Blue making it be treated as a fact. Repetition done over the years can help build a tradition such as Coca-Cola Coke is associated with family gatherings. Similarly, having Gillette Blue may be associated with masculinity and class, which becomes a sort of transition. The qualities that make a message easily recallable include precision, conciseness, improvisation, and alignment with the ideal family or society.

Secondly, keep the message brief and simple. As suggested, an advert is often run as a distraction and should be brief but packed with complete information. An advert can be purely audio or audiovisual. In whatever form that an advert is rendered, it should be brief and complete. An advert is an opportunity to remind people about the existence of a product and its features and the message should be brief to enable them easily memorize the contents. A simple and brief message enables the audience to easily memorize the advert after a few weeks of running. Even though it is possible to run an advert in sequences until the full picture develops the best way is to present the advert in summarized form.

As such, use simple language that is free of jargon. When running an advert, the intention is to reach the masses and not the schooled individuals only. The message contained in an advert should be easily deciphered devoid of ambiguities. For this reason, take the time to ensure that the right diction is infused in the advert. An advert should not leave the audience in suspense or require further analysis to understand what the advertiser wants to communicate. When building an advert, develop it along with common themes that the target audience can relate to. Some of the common themes include family love, protection for a child and living a colorful life.

Thirdly, build on popular lingo and mantra. Most people easily connect with popular phrases and slangs. Some of these phrases are extracted from tidbits of news, songs, and movies. As an advertiser, exploit these catchphrases to infuse them into your advert without losing the focus of the advert. Using popular lingo helps project the advertiser as trendy and creative. Using mantra in adverts makes the advertiser appear as connected and updated with current happenings in the country. Popular musicians and sporting icons are a rich source of popular lingo and mantra that the audience can easily identify with. However, when using borrowed catchphrases it is important to consider any implied violation of copyright.

Additionally, make the advert connected to life, love, and wellness. People value certain themes irrespective of age. Such themes include a masculine man showing care and love to a woman. The other popular themes that people identify with is adults feeling entertained by the innocence of children. People also identify with themes that advocate for caring for pets especially pet dogs. All these popular themes should be used when building an advert to widen the influence of the message. An advertiser that incorporates these themes in the advert is likely to reach a wider audience and have a lasting impact.

Against this backdrop, chances are that you prefer and remember adverts that elevate the value of family, respect, and care for children. The good thing is that these themes can be incorporated in almost all adverts. It is for this reason that children and family occupy a critical position in advertising. The masses are likely to show preferences for products that are perceived to contribute to a family setting, family values, care for children and care for pets. The reason for this attitude is that people identify the ideal life or humanity with these domains of life.

If one wants to achieve a lasting influence in running adverts then make the theme of family central. People do not just watch or listen to adverts but will seek to live them. However, when incorporating popular themes in adverts caution should be taken not to lose the focus of the advert especially if the product does not explicitly align with the selected theme. For instance, when making an advert about a brand of cement and incorporating love it is important not to make the advert about love but cement. For instance, such an advert can have a girlfriend showing a preference for fast-drying cement, which incorporates care for a woman and at the same time, captures the core message, which is a fast-drying cement brand.

Arguably true, one should use endorsement in building adverts. Using endorsements is akin to appealing to authority in persuasion. The young audience admires and dutifully follows their idols such as sportspersons and musicians. When such a celebrity is seen with any product then the followers will take that as a cue to switch to the celebrity's reference product. Companies such as Nike, Addidas, and Pepsi enlist the services of celebrities to endorse their products. For instance, if your favorite wrestler is seen with a particular energy drink then chances are that you will switch to the product because you are convinced that is the source of the magical strength.

Equally important, create your advert to be entertaining. People like adverts that are entertaining and this improves the memorability of such adverts. Chances are that you find entertaining adverts memorable and fun to watch. Another advantage of making adverts entertaining is that it frees you up to incorporate diverse elements without necessarily having a theme. A good example is the Coca-Cola Company that incorporates both family themes and entertainment in most of its adverts, which enhances the memorability of such adverts. For instance, the "Taste the feeling" advert campaign by Coca-Cola incorporates family themes and entertainment, which makes the advert fun to listen to and watch.

Another important aspect when seeking to influence through adverts is to enforce cultural competence. The contemporary world is diverse and any social interaction of people is likely to have people of different sexes, gender, ethnicities, religious affiliations, and socioeconomic status. Against the backdrop, companies have to invest more to ensure that the intended message is not lost in inadvertent accusations of discrimination or stereotypes. Most companies have to incorporate men and women, Caucasians and people of color, and different people from varying economic classes to ensure that each person in the audience feels accommodated. The messages and symbols used in adverts should not be easily linked to particular political, religious or radical groups.

Relatedly, emphasize the value that the product creates. When influencing through adverts, highlight the utility that the product is offering to customers. The utility could be real or perceptual but the most important thing is to highlight to current and potential customers. For example, the Coke soft drink can be sold as offering a refreshing taste, evoking memories, completing meals, and quenching thirst. All these real and perceptual features make the product's utility go up. Emphasizing on the features of a particular product can help differentiate the product in the market and increase the influence of such a product.

Against this backdrop, ensure that the previous, current and future messages are connected. Even though some companies overlook the need to make all their adverts connected, it is important to ensure that customers feel connected when being hit adverts from the company about the same product. Again, using the Coke adverts, most of them are connected and tend to signal an increase in features or utilization of the soft drink offering. Making adverts linked to each other helps underscore the intended message of the advertiser. Making advert messages can enhance the consistency of the adverts and improve the repetition feature of adverts.

Equally important, one should present the human face of the organization producing the product. As earlier on discussed, customers want to meet a human face when interacting with any business. Customers do not just want the product but also the experience. For this reason, adverts run by a business should exhibit a human face to enable customers to relate more with the message of the company. The other way of exhibiting human face by a business is to highlight any corporate social responsibility programs including emphasizing more on environmental sustainability programs that the company implements.

As expected, do not exaggerate the value created by using the product more than necessary. It is important when advertising not to promise what the product cannot deliver. For instance, if advertising a detergent does not just state that it is five times improved when it is not. Customers will feel cheated and in some cases, it may amount to false advertising. Adverts exaggerate but the overstating should be within acceptable ranges since customers may feel offended and abandon the product and any other offering by the company.

Chapter 13: Influence on religion

Religion is another sphere of life where influence is much needed. Adherents of religions want to expand their influence and recruit more people as well as retain current members. Religion is powerful, influences governments, and in some instances overrules governments. Over the centuries, religion has placed limits on scientific research and religious outfits have defeated systems of government and governments. Most people identify first with religion before identifying with their country and this indicates how powerful religion is in life.

Notably, appeal to authority and in this case, it is the deity that you worship, the holy book or another gifted minister. Concerning religion, people easily respect sources of authority such as holy books, which enables them to submit and obey your statements. Quoting a verse when making a statement will improve the weight of your assertions. Most major religions clergymen quote various verses from their holy books, which make the homily weighty. If you have attended church, you often heard your preacher or priest quote a book and verse, which adds authority to what he or she will discuss. The advantage of invoking the source of authority is that one is elevated before discussing what he or she wants to present.

An advantage of invoking authority in religion is that people have already readied their minds for receiving any message that their figure of authority delivers through an appointed person. Invoking an authority may also include referencing to another clergyman that has contributed significantly to the spread of faith or community service. Compared to the other domains of influence that we have discussed, it is easier to exert influence in religion, as most people do not require validated evidence to believe what they are being told. Additionally, most members of the congregation would happily become mini-influencers at the end of the service by expounding further, what was spoken by the speaker.

Equally important, you should appeal to tradition. Religion like culture has an established tradition that most members readily identify with and want to uphold. The tradition includes the way of dressing, pecking order, salutations and sitting arrangements among other attributes. A good influencer would share these traditions by observing them, which would endear the speaker to the target audience. The congregation will find a guest speaker that demonstrates a basic understanding of their tradition as being respectful and interested in their faith. For instance, if you can dress like a Muslim when going to speak in a function that is Islamic may endear you more to the audience than the contrary.

On the contrary, going to make an appearance at these functions and violating the tradition may ruin your chances of making a good first impression. For instance, not standing up and giving way when a Catholic priest walks by may be treated as the biggest form of disrespect to adherents of the Catholic faith. Lack of observing the tradition of the target audience concerning their faith will spoil the first impression of the audience of the speaker. For this reason, start doing a quick overview of the traditions of the target audience to help you plan and act accordingly.

Against this backdrop, one should lead by example if you intend to impress a congregation. Unlike the other domains such as politics, the congregation has high moral expectations of any speaker reminding them about their religious dogma. For instance, Catholics have high moral expectations of their priests and nuns and this requires that these figures of influence lead by example. Protestant churches have high ethical expectations of their bishops and reverends and they expect the figures of influence to act in a caring manner, honest way, and legal manner compared to the rest of the population. For this reason, you should lead by example to widen the sphere of influence in a religious context.

For emphasis, leading by example includes being consistent in what you say and do. For instance, it could be about punctuality, respecting others or donating to the less fortunate members of society. It may seem living a rehearsed life but a leader or an influencer in a religious context has some aspects of life delimited such as freely expressing his or her views on race, sex, and sexuality. The congregation will judge an influencer in the religious settings if he or she freely expresses sexuality, especially sexual orientation. For this reason, an ordained person leading by example may amount to living a rehearsed life.

Relatedly, one should make members of the congregation feel valued. As we argued earlier, all human beings desire to feel appreciated and loved. For this reason, you should start by appreciating the attendance and attention of members of the congregation. It is these little things that matter most. One should go further and emphasize the value of members of the gathering as dictated by the particular holy book. Most holy books of various religions describe the value and role of the members of the congregation which they easily identify with. A good influencer should make all members feel comfortable and appreciated.

Concerning making a lasting impact, an influencer should occasionally call certain members by their names as well as using any one of them in positive examples. When you mention members of the audience by their names or appearance in a positive manner the rest feel appreciated and perceive the influencer as interested in their lives. Making people feel valued also includes acknowledging their challenges and efforts. Most people turn up to religion when faced with uncertainty and making them aware that they know their challenges will help them become more interested in listening to what you have to offer.

Correspondingly, one should show empathy. As earlier indicated showing, empathy requires that you first understand your emotions and safely express manage. You should first understand common forms of emotions and how to safely manifest emotions before appreciating how others feel and react when faced with similar emotions. All these developments relate to empathy. Even though there various aspects of empathy, having the ability to read and adjust to the way one is feeling emotionally is highly desired. While reading emotions can be a challenge, fortunately, the body language of an individual can provide a convincing overview of the emotional status of the individual as we have insignificant control over our nonverbal communication.

Additionally, empathy includes placing oneself in the position of the other person. For instance, you should not encourage people to work hard when they are feeling demoralized. If people are feeling uninspired then no amount of resources given to them will make them become more productive or value the little they have. Before addressing an audience, you should try to establish the dominant emotion of the audience. If members are feeling uncertain and depressed then the diction of the message and the tone of voice should seek to reassure and usher in hope. Overall, empathy requires first understanding oneself and then understanding the position of others to help you become a caring and understanding friend.

As with any activity that involves communication, one should communicate clearly when addressing a congregation. When speaking to a group of people, you should assess their demographics in terms of their age, sex, gender, socioeconomic status, and literacy levels. Armed with the complete demographics of the audience, you should package your message to ensure that it reaches as many people as possible. Usually, you should use simple and standard language when addressing the audience to enable the majority of them to listen to connect with your message. The message should be brief where possible and summarize at the end for easy remembering.

Closely related to communicating clearly, ensure that the flow of communication is systematic by using transition words. Transition words include words such as firstly, secondly, additionally, for emphasis, and in summary among others. The role of transition phrases is to enable the audience to understand when an addition is made as well as when a contradiction is being made. It is common and acceptable for part of the audience to occasionally get lost when a presentation is being made and transition words enable the audience to quickly recover and catch-up with the intended overall message.

Equally important, manage the quality and flow of information to elevate your value as an influencer. A person that has the anticipated information is highly sought and listened to. When addressing an audience, only offer what is necessary and this should include limiting the time that you address the audience. Familiarity lowers the value of an influencer. An influencer should limit the information given which makes the audience eager to hear and act on future bits of information that they need. However, controlling the flow of information does not mean hoarding information, as this will only create room for others to exploit and create confusion.

For emphasis, most members of the audience are likely to be diverse even though they are united by religious teachings. It is still important to exercise restraint and accommodate others when making an address. For instance, members of the congregation are likely to e of different sex, gender, ethnicity, and socioeconomic status. Such members need to respect acceptance and comfort and any unsavory comments will make them feel displaced and lead to murmurs and exodus of members. Closely related, one should invoke group dynamics and use them to influence. People in a group are likely to mimic any actions of the influencer in a group without much deliberation. For this reason, an influencer should place people in various groups and use the group dynamics to widen the influence.

Chapter 14: Provide knowledge ethically dealing with other people's emotions.

One of the most challenging aspects of life is handling other people's emotions. Emotions are diverse and for this context, emotions are a form of energy created by the body to communicate to you how your overall body status is and you should allow this energy to dissipate. When the body status is composed, you will feel energized, happy and excited. The positive energy will be expressed by tears of joy, eagerness and lengthened the period of patience. On the other hand, when your body status is feeling threatened and unease you are going to express that energy in the form of fear, anger, and impatience. In this manner, emotional intelligence is about learning to acknowledge your emotions and finding a way to safely release them rather than blocking them. Most people wrongly think that negative emotions are unwanted when in the real sense, they are part of the human experience and what is required is to find a safe way to release that energy without harming others.

Notably, emotional intelligence influences your thoughts and actions to enable you to have control over your behavior as well as develop to handle it more effectively. With good levels of emotional intelligence, you will increase the way you identify and handle your emotions as well as how you react to the feelings of others. By becoming more emotionally stable, it allows us to grow and gain a comprehensive understanding of which we are and this allows us to communicate better with others and sustain stronger relationships. The following suggestions will give a good beginning point to discover the pillars of your emotional intelligence.

First, start by practicing noting how you feel. Your individual feelings will affect how you process and react to the feelings of the other person. Let us take a case where you have a loan to service and the business you invested in the loan is struggling. You are now working more than 10 hours a day to make extra income to sustain your lifestyle and also save some to service the loan. Due to frequent burnouts, you sometimes shout at your children when they play music at full volume. At the grocery store, you are easily irritated when the seller mixes up the groceries you selected. When driving home, you tend to experience road rage wondering how some drivers got their driving license. When online you easily pick up arguments with people that seem ignorant of what is being discussed. In this manner, you are highly emotional and may have issues processing the emotions of others.

Secondly, take note of how you react when processing the emotions of others to determine weak points and improve. You noticed right that we are focusing on you rather than the other person and the reason is that you can control your emotions and associated reactions but cannot fully manage those of the other person. When you understand how you react to different emotions manifested by different people, you can target to manage your reactions to attain predictability. Dealing with the emotions of other people requires first understanding how you react to negative and positive emotions. Emotions are largely a function of experience and society defined expectations. For instance, if you grew up in a society that does not allow a child to challenge an adult then when a student insults you there are chances that you will react extremely.

Thirdly, interrogate your opinions. In most cases, we form emotions because of the process that we have been given against an established history and spectra of meaning. For instance, if I make faces at you there is a chance that you will feel that I am taking you casually or mocking you. You interpreted by gestures by tapping into a stored knowledge and experience of established meaning of certain behaviors. Sometimes we would have acted differently if we paused and interrogated our opinions. We tend to react impulsively because that is what produces the best feeling but it is not the best way to navigate emotions thrown at us.

Fourthly, become accountable to your feelings. A common weakness that most people make is to provide excuses for their behaviors. For instance, you probably heard your colleague justify their behavior because the other person provoked. Justifying your reactions to the emotions of others will never help you to accept that you erred and need to fix your emotional intelligence competencies. Start by being accountable to your feelings and you will realize that you have significant space to improve on your weaknesses. Just because another person provoked you does not imply that you fall for it. One should develop the resilience that enables you to navigate emotive issues.

Additionally, practice deep breathing. Most people read and know what deep breathing is but rarely practice it. The logic behind urging deep breathing is to help convert the emotional energy into physical energy and thus defuse the intense reaction. When feeling agitated or targeted by the emotions of the other person, stand upright or sit upright and draw in a lot of air and expel it slowly letting you feel relieved. Repeat the exercise of relaxing the chest muscles and drawing in large gulps of air and expelling the air slowly by ensuring that your body feels the breath being expelled from the body. Even though this exercise may seem trivial, it is highly critical in helping navigate intense reactions.

In an attempt to improve, maintain a diary of your emotions and the matching reactions. Most people wrongly assume that they understand their emotions but in reality, they do not understand their emotions. An effective and simple way to understand your emotions is to maintain a diary of emotions.

For instance, capture the day, description of the emotion and how you reacted to the mentioned emotion. You will notice that there is a pattern in the manner that you react to certain situations, which implies such situations, and associated emotions can be predicted. Armed with this knowledge one can prepare in a safe way of expressing the emotions.

Correspondingly, let the emotions flow through you by taking it easy. When interacting with another person view the situation as that of a call center agent handling an emotive customer. As a call center agent, if you absorb the emotions thrown at you there are chances that you will end up feeling frustrated and overwhelmed by the job. The safest bet when handling the emotions of another person is to allow those emotions to flow through you. Let us take the case of a customer care desk at the fictitious company. If a dejected customer shows up and shouts at you, you will not take the reaction as directed you but rather the organization you present. If your friend expresses intense negative emotions, you should treat the emotion as directed as someone else that the friend wants you to represent because you will understand the situation.

Relatedly, accept when your emotions are triggered and safely express them. A common mistake most people make is to think that masking emotions equate to maturity and stability. Most individuals consider expressing negative emotions as something to be ashamed of as it contradicts the perfect image that people want. However, all emotions including the negative ones should be expressed. What matters is how safely one expresses these emotions. For instance, if your friends feel upset and shout at you there is a likelihood that you may also respond similarly. If one cannot absorb the emotions of a friend, you must manifest your response including negative emotions.

As earlier on suggested define your limits and exert your position. Most people fear to exert their position because of being labeled as hardliners or inconsiderate. However, this is a fallacy, exerting your views enables define boundaries and makes your friends understand your limits. When confronted with emotions from friends, you should make it clear that your limits are to enable the friend to understand when you can snap or walk away from the social interaction. Think of a situation where you are arguing with a colleague and the colleague decides to start discussing your weaknesses. You should make it clear that your personal should be respected and that you will not allow further discussion of your personal life.

While empathizing, remember that it does amount to shouldering the burden of others. We discussed earlier that a mistake that most people commit is to attempt to carry the challenges of their friends. A person that is entangled with a friend and wants to absorb the burdens in the life of that friend is bound to feel used and exhausted shortly. When handling emotions from a friend, ensure that you do not transfer them to your personal life. You should only empathize as opposed to making those challenges part of your responsibility.

Learn to extricate oneself from emotions. Even though our lives and emotions are intricate, we can still extricate ourselves from emotions to realize an objective view of a situation. When confronted with emotions from a friend, we should try to view the situation devoid of our individual and the friend's emotions. Assessing a situation devoid of emotions can help you see the underlying issues and confront them for a lasting solution. For instance, a suddenly moody friend could be having difficulties servicing mortgage or having marital issues. Without dropping emotions, you would be stuck on the personality of your friend rather than probing the underlying causes of the sudden transformation.

You must listen to actively. In most cases, we get emotional because we fail to listen and understand what our friends are struggling to communicate. Since our friends have high expectations of us, they easily get frustrated when we fail to relate to their feelings. In this context, active listening involves exuding the appropriate body language to denote affirmation, refuting, and attention. A keen listener may read a lot from the choice of words used by another person as well as the body language to profile the current emotional status of the individual. Overall navigating emotions of a friend requires exuding emotional intelligence competencies.

Chapter 15: Tips and checklist to spot and stop manipulators.

Manipulators are suave and spotting one may not be easy. Most manipulators act subtly, which may take time before the victims of the manipulation understand what is happening. There is a possibility of someone manipulating others without realizing that he or she is manipulating. In some situations, manipulation may appear justified. For instance, workers seeking a rise may engage in a go-slow to make the management appreciate their contribution to the growth of the organization. However, in this chapter, we will focus on manipulators that are aware of their intent and whose actions are deemed unethical.

They appeal to emotions even where it is not necessary

Most manipulators will invoke emotions in situations that should be neutral in terms of emotions. The dalliance with emotions is that emotions cloud objective judgment and makes people vulnerable to half-truths and biases. When angry, one is likely to speak without moderation and this can trigger further conflicts considering that most social gatherings are full of diversity. Manipulators like such an environment where one can exploit emotive issues to accomplish sinister motives. Think of a colleague who takes a miscommunication from the management to make it look like the organization is against women's empowerment and proceeds to incite female workers to sabotage the productivity of the organization.

They exploit any differences to their advantage

Apart from appealing to emotions, manipulators will tap into differences to accomplish their self-serving goals. Most workplaces and social events are full of diversity manifested in terms of different genders, sexes, ethnicities and socioeconomic statuses. A determined manipulator will negatively emphasize the diversity either explicitly or subtly. Even though there is progress concerning being open-minded and respectful of other people based on their race, sex and ethnicity among others there is still simmering biases and discriminations. Against this backdrop, without well-intentioned people, there is bound to be discrimination and biases and this is what manipulators want. Manipulating people requires having a significant number of them feeling that they matter more compared to the rest.

They do not give you a choice

As expected, manipulators understand that they have limited time to influence people before they are exposed. For this reason, a manipulator will want to exhaust everything given an opportunity. On the other hand, an influencer will willingly allow adequate time to persuade the target audience. A manipulator may not want the target audience to have adequate time to rationalize what is being said and for this reason, manipulators hit the audience with successful loads of information and misinformation. Think of a manipulator as a hawker determined to make you purchase their wares, he or she will ensure that you are fully engaged to force impulsive reasoning.

They persist even where all the members agreed to compromise and move forward

As indicated, a manipulator thrives more where differences and conflicts exist. A manipulator seeks to turn one side against the other and use each of the sides to accomplish sinister motives. For this reason, when a manipulator notices a compromise he or she will seek to reactivate the conflict and differences while pretending to be innocent. Most manipulators are observant and assess the personality of each member of the target audience. Manipulators will make a move that will help trigger and fester conflicts and biases to ensure that there are plenty of emotions within the target audience.

They are not interested in recruiting the majority but only a few

Unlike influencers, most manipulators are disinterested in having everyone subscribe to their sinister motives. Most manipulators' intent is to attain persuasion within the shortest time possible and for this reason; they focus more on the high-value select individual in the organization. A manipulator will identify a potential figure of influence and sell their sinister goals to the person. Once a manipulator gets a threshold number of subscribers then he or she will immediately implement the self-serving plan while the rest believe that the suggestions will help improve their welfare. In other terms, a manipulator is disinterested in the welfare of all but only his or her vested interests.

Where possible they issue threats

Manipulators issue veiled and explicit threats that are meant to instantly convince others into submission. People that issue threats intend to prevent questions since any form of interrogation will expose the manipulator. Threats are preferred since they help attain fast results within the shortest time through the effects wear off almost immediately. Additionally, threats deny the victim free will and make the person scared of the consequences even when the trigger is withdrawn. Threats tend to dehumanize the victim. For instance, a manipulator may state that if you fail to belong to the mentioned group then you risk being labeled a traitor which is a veiled threat that the manipulator will turn others against you.

Where possible they play victims

When cornered, manipulators will play victim to avoid being reprimanded. Since most of the actions of manipulators are self-serving and exploit diversity at the workplace, most manipulators feel embarrassed when exposed. For this reason, most manipulators do not just play victims but will still manipulate others to feel that they are victims. By making everyone feel targeted, manipulators attain a perfect shield of being held accountable. Think of a student who takes advantage of issues with security at school to incite others to boycott classes. Once such a student realizes that the administration is on his case, he will make it appear like anyone that criticizes the administration is marked for suspension and make his problems, everyone's issue.

They are impatient and want maximum results within a short period

A manipulator is a scheming person and will want quick results. For this reason, most manipulators focus on short-term activities with high impact as far persuading people are concerned. Unlike influencers, manipulators will not belabor with building philosophies as these take time and require working with all the people. Manipulators will not seek to establish lasting relationships and interactions because they do not harbor long-term agenda with the welfare of the audience. Deploying manipulation tactics, in the long run, is infeasible as people are likely to expose the manipulator and disengage completely.

Stopping manipulators

Define your limits and freewill

Making a potential manipulator understand your boundaries and freewill will enable him or her understand that you are aware of the self-serving attempts. The best way to stem any attempt of manipulation is to preempt by making it known that you loathe being manipulated. If someone knows that you can anticipate and defend oneself against any manipulation they are likely to drop the idea altogether. Setting boundaries helps make each of the people understand the sensitive areas and what makes the other person uncomfortable. Think of a friend that first informs people that he dislikes liars and manipulators.

Chances are that any manipulator will avoid attempting manipulation.

Read attempts to manipulate you especially through body language

Fortunately, we can predict attempts to manipulate us by analyzing body language. Most people that manipulate will either prolong eye contact or avoid eye contact which suggests insincerity. Some manipulators would speak with a low voice to evoke calmness to help make their victims feel calm. Some manipulators will use rehearsed body language that aligns with their message to persuade the audience. Against this backdrop, scout for any suspect body language and any disconnect between verbalized message and the nonverbal message. One of the common tactics of manipulators is to mimic the body language of the target victim to mind control them.

Read any attempts to play the victim

As indicated, most manipulators play the victim as a safe bet when they feel threatened. Children are some of the best manipulators when given chance and will play the victim cared when faced with consequences. A manipulator reads any attributes of diversity and weaponized it. For instance, a manipulator will exploit the difference in genders to create an impasse. A manipulator will take advantage of different ethnicities at the workplace to pity one against the other and then use both of them to accomplish self-serving interests. For instance, a manipulator may exploit the diversity in terms of ethnicities to trigger leadership changes at the organization.

Read any attempt to dwell on personal descriptions of everyone Expectedly, most manipulators seek to exploit any source of emotional feelings and this includes personalizing everything. Most manipulators will try to guide discussions into making personal comments to help trigger emotions. As indicated, emotions help manipulators easily flourish as emotions cloud judgment. If one is extremely excited or angry chances are that you make impulsive decisions devoid of consideration of long-term effects of such decisions. A manipulator schemes for such a moment as people will not probe the messaging of a manipulator. Think of a politician that harbors radical views and seizes an opportunity when insecurity incidents increase and the masses are angrily demanding for robust security measures to push for leftist laws.

Detect any inconsistency

Manipulator actions closely align with liars even though he or she is not necessarily one. A manipulator lacks consistency but it takes a keen eye to detect the inconsistency because it is projected as consistency. Most politicians are manipulators and can best illustrate the inconsistency disguised as consistency. For instance, a politician will shift positions based on prevailing emotions but make it fit within his or her loosely defined leadership philosophy. For most people, they will see consistency but in a real sense, the politician is inconsistency and uses a loosely defined leadership philosophy as a perfect mask of the inconsistency. By detecting any significant deviations one can suspect manipulation.

Set consequences

Defending oneself against manipulation requires making the manipulator understand the consequences of exploitation and lying. Chances are that if a manipulator is aware that the target person loathes inconsistency and exploitation then the manipulator will abort the scheme. When you suspect manipulation, make your manipulator understand that you will not take manipulation kindly.

Chapter 16: How to detect deception

All of us would want to easily determine deception at any level such as personal, social and organizational levels but it is not that easy. Some professions that rely wholly on determining the truth in personal and social contexts such as law agencies, health agencies, and media agencies invest heavily in determining the truth value of their productions but they fairly fail despite having immense resources. Since human behavior is dynamic, detecting dynamic is not easy as they are bound to be false positives.

However, there is only one reliable way to determine deception and that is creating a baseline for the target individual and comparing against this baseline as well as doing the adequate prior investigation before confronting the person. Unfortunately, establishing a baseline for each and conducting relevant background study is not always assured due to the time factor and resource constraints and this implies that a speedy analysis of body language and verbal communication can help determine a likelihood of a truth or a lie.

Focus on verbal cues

First, liars tend to respond to questions that were not asked. If one is lying then he or she wants to cover as much ground as possible and this includes answering questions that were not posed. By responding to questions that were not asked, the individual is prompting the speaker to a particular direction and does not want to be caught off guard. Answering questions that are not asked may also give the individual lying an opportunity to deny the speaker adequate time to analyze the answers given by continuously bombarding the interrogator with new information and ideas. Lastly answering questions that were not asked also helps the layperson to appear well prepared and knowledgeable in what is being asked.

Secondly, most liars tend to answer a question with a question. Expectedly, most liars will respond to a question with another question to shift the burden of thinking and responding to the interrogator. Most politicians employ this tactic when being interviewed and it is meant to buy them enough time to recall information to the main question. For most liars, not responding is akin to affirming that they lack memory of what is being asked or what happened. The other purpose of responding to a question with another question is to irritate the interrogator and derail his or her composure. Responding to a question with a question is a defensive tactic indicating attempts to hide something.

Thirdly, most liars tend to make self-corrections to avoid sounding uncertain. As indicated, most liars want to ensure that each area is covered to eliminate any doubts because allowing room for doubt may expose them. For this reason, most liars tend to self-correct to ensure the information given is irrefutable. In most cases, liars will repeat the correction to ensure that the interrogator and the audience also capture the self-correction. As expected, the liar will blame the need to self-correct on a slip of the tongue or the fast nature of the interview. Another reason for self-correction by a liar is that the individual has a premeditated script and outcome and keeps forcing everything to align with the premeditated picture.

Fourthly, liars tend to feign memory loss. As expected, most liars need a safe exit when cornered and feigning memory loss is a favorite excuse for most liars. When a liar is cornered then he or she will cite memory loss and later institute self-correction to attain the preformed script. Try watching interviews with politicians to appreciate how they feign memory loss to escape explaining something and pretend to have recalled the information when there is an opportunity to sound believable.

Additionally, most liars tend to report what they did not do as opposed to what they did.
People that lie will give an account of what they did not do to avoid being held accountable. If a liar dwelled on what he or she did then the individual can be held accountable and this is not something that a liar wants. However, if a liar dwells on what they should have done then he or she has a large degree of

freedom to give any answer and avoid scrutiny. Again, try watching a recorded or filed interview with any politician to appreciate how this technique is employed.

Expectedly, most people practicing deception tend to justify their actions even when not necessary. As such, most liars are insecure and are uncertain that they are sounding convincing. For this reason, they over-justify everything because they feel that no one believes them even when people have fallen for the lies. When examining a potential liar, look for signs of unnecessary justification and again politicians will provide a good case study of over-justification.

Relatedly, most liars avoid mentioning emotional feelings in their version of events. Since a liar is faking everything, he or she will avoid mentioning emotional feelings that were associated with what is being reported. Mentioning emotional feelings may force one to show them. For instance, if you talking about an exciting event that you witnessed then your facial expressions and voice should manifest positive emotions and this is not something a liar wants because he or she is not assured of consistency of verbal communication and body language.

Correspondingly, most liars are careful and will insist on a question to be repeated. Liars focus more on what is being asked because they only want to accept a question that they are certain of responding to. Liars dwell more on what the question is and what the interrogator wants to help them generate convincing information. The other role of wanting questions repeated is to help the liar elicit a response by making up one because there is none.

Focusing on body language

An individual attempting deception will likely randomly throws gestures. The hand gestures are among the best indicator of positive and negative emotions and are difficult to fake in a consistent manner. If one is angry but is pretending to be calm, he or she will throw gestures randomly. Most liars get irritated when taken to the task of what they just said and are likely to throw random gestures in the air even as they try to sound calm.

Against the norm, he or she speaks first than usual. People that normally do not speak fast will suddenly speak fast when they are lying. Speaking fast helps, the person denies the audience adequate time to listen and analyze the information. Speaking fast also allows the liar to exhaust all of the rehearsed information, as any interjection will throw the liar off the balance. Speaking fast also indicates that the person is uncomfortable with the audience or the message and wants to finish fast and end the experience.

Relatedly, he or she sweats more than usual. People sweat and it is normal. However, more than normal levels of sweating even when the weather is fine may indicate that one is panicking and feeling cornered. All these may indicate a sign of a liar.

Additionally, a liar avoids eye contact. Most liars shun eye contact or give a sustained stare to intimidate the target person. Shunning eye contact indicates that the person feels awkward or embarrassed with what he or she is presenting to the audience. If one paces up and down more than necessary then the individual is likely lying. All these indicate feeling uncomfortable with the message and the audience.

Chapter 17: Tips and workout to increase self-esteem in order to avoid being manipulated

The shortcomings of most books on building self-esteem are that they do not approach the issue from the fundamentals. Low self-esteem has underlying causes that include an unfortunate childhood. Most of the provided solutions out here focus on guiding the individual when he or she is already interacting but in this chapter; we focus on helping one build the mental stamina at the mind-level before venturing out. For this reason, fixing low self-esteem requires helping the victim build social skills systematically. However, building social skills requires emotional intelligence competencies for one have to first become aware of how they feel and their emotional status before extending to the outside circle.

Regarding social skills, let us begin with survival skills. The specific competencies here include the following guidelines, listening, ignoring distractions and using brave talk as well as rewarding oneself. Social contexts might require you to follow instructions and overlook distractions. Not all people can ignore distractions as the human mind processes everything it can decipher. It is important to train your mind to act in a disciplined manner by avoiding distractions and sticking to the recommended guidelines. It is also important that you reward yourself to enable you to feel worth engaging in social interaction.

Secondly, one should build their interpersonal skills. The particular skills here include asking for permission, sharing, waiting your time, and joining an activity. It takes the experience to know when to interrupt or join a conversation. In most cases, the range of required interpersonal skills depends on the context. The justification here is that the interpersonal skills you exercise when watching your favorite team play are not the same as the one you exhibit when with your colleagues at the workplace.

Thirdly, one should build problem-solving skills and specifically asking for help, accepting consequences, and apologizing. In social contexts, disagreements will occur and at the same time, the parties in the interaction might require your input to resolve an issue. A socially competent individual needs to identify the underlying causes of the problem, how it is affecting others, why the rest of the people are feeling the way they are, and finally offering impartial and multiple ways of fixing it.

Fourthly, one should hone conflict resolution skills and specifically handling loses, accusations, peer pressure, and dealing with flatter. Resolving conflicts is a highly demanded skill in contemporary society that is increasingly diverse. Solving conflicts require being impartial, empathically listening and helping the feuding parties acknowledge their shared ground on the issue. Unresolved conflicts can end social interactions and at the workplace affect productivity in several ways. For instance, unresolved conflicts can make some workers quit a certain team or leave the organization altogether.

Additionally one should possess the ability to persuade and influence others. In social contexts, one should possess the ability to convince others. Influencing others relies on emotional intelligence competencies especially empathy and emotional value communication. When you understand the emotional impact of the words in your communication then it becomes easier to use it to win others. Persuading people also means that you appreciate how they feel and take into account when communicating with them.

Relatedly, one should develop leadership skills. Within social contexts, sometimes one has to show leadership. Within a group, it will require a leader or a dominant member and possessing leadership skills is part of social skills. A good leader inspires and listens while being visionary. When participating in social contexts, it is important that you cultivate leadership skills and demonstrate them where appropriate. One of the preferred models of leadership is the transformative leadership where the leader motivates the members rather than commanding or setting the pace for the team.

Notably one should exhibit communication skills that operationalize social skills. As expected, communication skills are essential in any social activity. Some of the communication skills required include the effective use of nonverbal communication. It is important that the facial expressions and gestures used are appropriate and at the same time tally with verbal communication. Groups are likely to be diverse and hand gestures might have different connotations for each member involved. For this reason, communication should also include cultural competencies.

Additionally one should build bonds that are requisite for social skills. Part of social interactions is developing relationships. Creating a relationship will also require a skill to sustain the relationship. Not all people can initiate and sustain a relationship. The competence of building and sustaining relationships is part of the social skills that one must possess. Empathy is a critical competence when building and managing a relationship. Building and handling relationships is largely an art but following best practices increases chances of succeeding.

Correspondingly, change management skills are a critical part of social skills. Another continuous aspect of social interactions is changing. In any group setting, one or several members might leave or behave differently than the known behavioral set and these calls for change management competencies to avert fallouts in the group.

It is also important to tag along with the normal success curve. One of the major triggers of self-esteem is adjusting expectations to unrealistic levels and then struggling to attain and sustain the ridiculous standards. Learn to accept realistic expectations as the ideal yardstick of success. When you normalize your expectations, you are likely to feel satisfied and may internalize success. The realistic levels also imply that the expended energy is within the normal range and this can prevent fatigue and anxiety. When you adjust your targets to the expected range then you are likely to start accepting yourself and your capabilities, which may initiate you into social life. Lowering your expectations of performance is necessary to break the vicious cycle of self-esteem issues.

As such, you should adjust your efforts and ambitions to realistic levels as part of the normal success. For emphasis, revise down your ambitious targets to the ones that you can attain. Start with the average ambitions and expectations and scale up gradually. It is not easy for a person with self-esteem issues to revise down their targets. Maintaining the ridiculous high target enables the person to feel unsettled, unworthy and motivated to prove oneself. For most affected people, the ridiculous high targets are necessary to help them finally prove their worth but the cycle never stops. One of the ways of ensuring the applicability of this recommendation cut your current targets by a quarter percentage and subsequently reduces the new lower target until it matches the organizational average.

Relatedly, concentrate on accomplishing the tasks rather than outshining everyone because this is the other push factor for setting unrealistic expectations. The motivation for defining unrealistic expectations is because you want to be outstanding. When you get preoccupied with being among the best then your energy and efforts are not on emotional needs or the impact of the solution you are creating but rather you are in a race with people who are unaware they are competing with you. Since you are in a perpetual race with others who are largely unaware that you are competing with them, you have to set your targets higher than everyone else to stay ahead of them does. When doing all these, you are forgetting that you forcing your mind and body to use the energy and efforts of all the people you want to outshine aggravating your productivity output and overall health.

One should embrace marginal improvement in success. At some point, you will need to improve and it is advisable that you go for marginal improvement. Sustained improvement is the hallmark of a productive and progressive worker. When setting new targets, set small, measurable and achievable ones. The pitfall of most individuals with self-esteem issues is that they want to attain a decade's worth of success in a year if not months. Everyone needs to gradually improve but the new level of delivering should be realistic. When an individual commits to deliver a higher level than previous then the person is seeking to maximize and optimize their skills and knowledge, which is beneficial for the individual and the organization. However, when such improvement costs the social skills and overall health of the individual then it is not worth the effort.

Against this backdrop, avoid going for wholesale improvement but instead go for specific areas to improve. The common mistake that persons with self-esteem issues make is that they do not segment and modularize the areas for improvement. Instead, persons with self-esteem issues go for wholesale improvement, which makes it difficult to realize small but critical aspects of improvement. Additionally, the wholesale approach to improvement means that the individual expends so much energy and resources creating risk for burnout, anxiety, and isolation. Indeed, some of the intentions of people with self-esteem issues are well-intentioned but the approach is flawed making the entire venture infeasible and costly.

Relatedly, allow yourself adequate time to make improvements in areas identified. Once you assess yourself and determine the weak areas, spread the change process over a considerable period of time. Some changes will occur in a week, a month, a year or even over five years period. It is ill-advised to pursue a five-year change need in just a month. It might be necessary to share with others or seek professional help to help you pursue a change to fix your weakness over a reasonable period. For instance, punctuality can be improved within a month but public speaking may require an entire year to fully improve.

One should also accept failure. Learn to accept failure as a normal process and failure does not mean weakness. Not all people have the competency to welcome and process failure. Most people struggle to pass negative feedback by feeling angry, unworthy or blaming themselves for failure. When you encounter failure, accept that it is inevitable. Then conduct an evaluation to determine the internal and external factors that precipitated the failure. Identify your contribution to that failure in a fair manner and accept responsibility for your contribution. With all these developments, develop lessons from the failure incident. When you learn to treat failure as a source of learning then you increase the will and competency of processing failure.

Equally important, appreciate that you cannot control all factors when handling a task. As part of accepting failure, you will realize that there are external and internal factors that affect the delivery of any task. By accepting accountability up to where you were responsible, it does not mean that you are masking or exonerating yourself from failure but you are being realistic. One of the lessons you will learn is that you must plan for unforeseen or uncontrollable factors by developing a contingency plan. Some controllable factors can become uncontrollable and this implies that having a contingency plan for controllable and uncontrollable is critical for delivery. For instance, your health is fairly manageable but it can quickly become unmanageable and there is a need to have a contingency plan for such.

In a group setting, learn to be accountable but also share the failure when it occurs. For persons with self-esteem, they consistently feel unworthy and misplaced even when contributing the most in a team setting. For this reason, affected persons will absorb all the blame on a group even when other members caused it and this is due to feeling that they were not their position in the first place. Apart from accepting failure at a personal level, it is also important to share it with others that participated in a joint activity.

When addressing self-esteem issues it is necessary that you acknowledge your strengths and weaknesses. Assess yourself to determine your strengths and weaknesses. As suggested previously, conduct an assessment of your areas of weaknesses and strengths. The assessment will help you appreciate that you cannot always deliver and each person must exhibit strengths and weaknesses. By evaluating your strengths and weaknesses, you will realize that you can leverage your strengths to minimize the effects of your weaknesses when working. For individuals with self-esteem, they unjustifiably dwell on real and imagined weaknesses and this makes such persons feel burdened to continuously validate themselves. By acknowledging your strengths, you will learn to start feeling satisfied with your achievements.

Relatedly using the assessment identifies the areas you are likely to deliver exceptionally. Once you conduct the assessment, you will note the areas that you are likely to excel in. Naturally, you will prefer taking tasks that fall within your strengths but this should not make you try challenging areas. The advantage of human weakness is that they can be unlearned or learned to improve and make them qualified strengths. When you identify your weaknesses, you will realize the importance of working with others or consulting. At the same time, you will use your strengths for the benefit of all rather than for self-gratification.

As such, accept new challenges and use your strengths and weaknesses to minimize failure. As suggested, take up new challenges, as these will help you work on your weak areas. Staying in your current position implies that you are avoiding showing your full whole by only showing your strengths. New challenges may also help you discover hidden strengths that you have that you did not exist. Similarly, new challenges might help you unearth unknown weaknesses that you did not know you had. For this reason, you should start entertaining the idea of taking up new tasks or asking for additional tasks where feasible.

Against this backdrop, acknowledge and celebrate your achievements. Learn to acknowledge and process any milestone you make. An individual with self-esteem issues, one has difficulties connecting the success to internal abilities and efforts. Start taking time to feel satisfied with each milestone that you make. Saying phrases such as "I thank you all that worked with me to enable me to deliver" or "It has been a journey but finally I have accomplished it" will help you feel connected to the accomplishments that you make. The other way of celebrating your achievements is to recognize that you were hired because of your merit and your delivery is standard. Reflection can also make you feel that you have come far to accomplish what you have.

Furthermore, learn to welcome and accept compliments. The difficulty with remaining in the moment and focusing on your strengths makes an individual with self-esteem issues feel that each accolade won is merely a flatter. When you attach your achievements to your efforts then you find reasons to feel that you deserve the awards or recognition. It all starts with you recognizing your efforts and contribution to a solution. When you price or value your efforts then you will increase the likelihood of feeling that you matter and have made an impact on a project. It might be necessary to debrief the individual of their unfortunate childhood to enable them to feel worthy of anything.

For emphasis, learn to feel satisfied when you achieve. Apart from accepting rewards and recognition, it is important that you learn to feel satisfied when you achieve. For persons with self-esteem issues, each success leaves them to feel inferior and worthless forcing them to even adjust their expectations of performance higher. By learning to feel content with the current achievement you will feel okay delivering at the realistic standards. You should try to feel that no one is after you or that they are people just waiting to prove that you are unqualified to hold your current position and start enjoying the processes and the moment.

Chapter 18: Illustrations of manipulation and ways of defending against it

Political messaging

All of us are routinely exposed to political messaging through mainstream media and social media. Politicians are skilled manipulators and exploit diversity to pity one side against the other. Areas of diversity such as gender, race, socioeconomic status, and sex easily provide triggers of intense emotions and distrust that makes it easier for a politician to influence the target group. Intense emotions also provide ground for lack of objective analysis of the political messaging. Politicians have vested interests and would want to attain maximum influence, using few people and the least amount of time, which fits the definition of manipulation according to this book.

For instance, a politician will wait for unfortunate news such as a shooting of a minority youth within a particular neighborhood to manipulate the public including the legislative house. Let us assume that police mistakenly shoot an unarmed African American teenager on suspicion of being involved in drug trafficking. If it happens that, the offending officer is Caucasian then this provides ground for politicians to whip up emotions along ethnicity lines. For instance, if the politician wants to pity the African American community against the dominant Whites then all he needs to do is to exploit the emotions to portray the African Americans as a targeted helpless community.

On the other hand, the same politician may exploit the mentioned situation to emphasize the stereotype that the majority of young African Americans are involved in crime and push for stiffer penalties against drug pushers without seeking to address the underlying socioeconomic causes of the trend. The same politicians may push for laws that delineate and make it difficult for minority communities in the neighborhood to integrate with others. All the politicians need to do is to exploit the simmering tension between the affected ethnicities to make each feel threatened and push for dominance through established frameworks.

Regarding defending oneself against political manipulation, it is necessary to establish the truth. Most politicians' present half-truths which the public fails to read through and use the exaggeration and misinformation. Taking time to probe the truth-value of the political statements made by politicians will deconstruct their lies. For this reason, one must always interrogate the factual basis of a political statement before believing it. It is also advisable to accept that politicians are inherent manipulators and always validate their claims.

Advertising

Even though most of the adverts have to exhibit some ethicality standards, some of the adverts put out reek of manipulation. Adverts are intended to make the public aware of a product, remind the masses of the product and its features, convince the public to embrace the product, and help the public differentiate the product from others and counterfeits. However, in some instances, some adverts employ manipulative tactics to accomplish instant influence and other self-serving interests. The advertiser, in that case, understands that the customers do not require the product but he or she is more interested in making sales and cares not what happens to impulsive buying of the product by customers.

For instance, you may have encountered a loan shark that wrongly influenced you to take up a loan that you clearly did not. The promoter of the loan product manipulated you as he or she was wholly interested in attaining the self-serving reason, which is to sell loan products and get a commission. Manipulation occurs where the customer is wrongly influenced to take up a product that he or she does not or does not get the utility defined. In this case, a customer has been manipulated. The person hawking the loan cares not that you may lag behind payments or get auctioned as long as he or she accomplished his target of selling a loan product. If the person selling the loan package were to be exposed, he or she would not be proud of what he or she did.

Regarding manipulation in advertising, one should read the fine print at the end of the advert or the product. Go further and compare with other existing products that serve the same purpose. However, the best way to protect oneself against manipulative advertising is to directly interrogate the terms and conditions of using the product. Any attempts by promoters to sell you a product without wanting to give you adequate time to make a decision could be an attempted manipulation and you should make them understand that you dislike manipulation and manipulators in equal measure.

Relationship conflicts

Some partners in relationships are good at manipulating their better halves. Relationships experience conflicts and this is normal as well unavoidable. Conflicts manifest due to differing views as well as the rich diversity in terms of gender, religious affiliations, political affiliations, personality, and ethnicity. Manipulators in relationships exploit any sensitive issue to make the other partner do something for them and prefer to play victims. What is interesting is that the manipulated partner may feel that he or she is an uncaring and cruel partner. Like all forms of manipulation, the victim of manipulation is likely to feel exhausted and worthless.

An example of manipulation of in a relationship is your partner accusing you of spending more time at work when you first notified him or her that during that month you will work more to accomplish a due project. A manipulative partner will not fulfill any of the agreed roles and upon putting the person to the task, he or she will remind you that it is you to blame. If these exchanges continue for days, you might start feeling that you are responsible for lack of your partner assisting kids do their homework, delays in paying for utilities and for lack of order at the household. However, your partner just manipulated you by exploiting the gender element of diversity in which he or she made you appear as someone who had absconded the society-influenced gender roles.

It is common in relationships for partners to explicitly use gender to shield themselves from assuming the responsibilities of their actions. There is a chance that when you try to hold your partner responsible for what he or she did that they will invoke their gender to make you appear insensitive and radical on understanding the gender of the affected partner. For instance, if you are a man and are trying to hold your wife accountable, there are significant chances that she will make it appear like you do not understand or respect women, which forces you to stop the exchange.

Regarding defending oneself against manipulation in a relationship you should read the body language of your partner more and make them understand that they are being unfair. Manipulating partner will likely exhibit body language such as gestures, facial expressions, and posture as well as the tone of voice that contradicts the verbal communication. When a partner voices that he or she is okay with your suggestion but his or her body language contradicts the verbal message then you should stick with the body language. Analyzing the alignment or disconnect between verbal communication and body language is critical in determining dishonest claims made by a partner.

Workplace manipulation

There are several instances of manipulation at the workplace but for this example, we will focus on supervisor manipulation of the subordinates. In line with all forms of manipulation, workplace manipulators want the maximum value of results within the shortest time possible. One form of manipulation at the workplace is to issue threats such as disciplinary measures, retrenchment, and transfer and a pay cut. The manipulator understands that workers do not want to invite any of these on themselves and will do anything to minimize facing the consequences of threats.

Apart from issuing threats, a supervisor at the workplace may also exploit the sources of diversity at the workplace to exert undue influence. For instance, a supervisor may rate the output of females and males differently which is meant to force men to work more than women by invoking stereotypes that men are better than women at the workplace. The supervisor may also use the same manipulation based on gender to quell any discontent by making women feel that they complain a lot, unlike men. A manipulator may also manipulate the workplace by playing employees against their ethnicities. For instance, a supervisor may state that he is proud of Hispanics who work more and complain less, which is meant to force others not to speak out as they currently are doing.

Regarding defending workplace manipulation, it is the most difficult to defend oneself against it. Most workplace manipulation can be easily qualified by the standard operating procedures of an organization as well as the code of conduct at the workplace. However, the best way to defend workplace manipulation is to courteously exert your rights and make the superior understand that you are protected from outright manipulation.

Chapter 19: Guide to dealing with bullying behavior

Bullying behavior exists beyond the school settings. Bullying behavior entails aggressive actions that deny the victim the freewill and sometimes dignity. Bullying behavior is accomplished through aggression, stereotypes, threats, violence, avoidance, enticement and sabotage among others. Bullying behavior is manifest in relationships, workplaces and in politics as well as in social events. In some instances, the individual perpetuating bullying behavior is largely unaware that they are perpetuating bullying behavior. It is necessary that one be armed with the competencies of defending against bullying behavior.

Stereotypes as a tool for bullying behavior

You can be bullied where the offending individual makes fun of your sex, ethnicity, religion, looks and economic status by invoking stereotypes. For instance, women are seen as highly emotional and lazy. African Americans are portrayed as lazy and oriented to crime including dysfunctional families. Hispanics are projected as oriented towards gang violence and reckless sex. Muslims are portrayed as thriving in religious extremism. All these stereotypes can make one feel uncomfortable and force the victim to act without freewill and feel misplaced.

Regarding defending oneself against stereotype as a tool of bullying behavior, one should speak out stereotyping and define limits. When interacting with friends, make it clear to them that you believe in mutual respect and accommodating of other people regardless of their ethnicity, economic status, sex, and religious affiliation. Exerting yourself is important to make the offending person understand that you will not entertain such behavior and actions.

Avoidance as a tool for bullying behavior

Sometimes an offending person bullies you indirectly by ensuring that you are isolated. For instance, a colleague could influence other workmates to simply avoid you, which will bully you into submission to the needs of the offending person. Think of walking into the office and all people suddenly pretending to be busy working but as soon you leave they manage to hold a hearty conversation and upon returning they suddenly go silent. Some people do not even understand that being isolated from others is bullying behavior.

Regarding tackling avoidance as a bullying behavior one should not compromise when they know they are right in accordance with the ethical code of conduct. Instead, ensure that you meet and speak to each of your workmates making them understand that you have no qualms but they should understand your position. With time, you will win back most of your colleagues.

Threats as a tool of bullying behavior

A common form of bullying behavior is issuing veiled and explicit threats. Veiled threats are communication that warns of dire consequences without using words that explicitly denote a threat. For instance, veiled threats can include things such as the organization prefers workers that score 45 on the appraisal report and at the moment, it is likely to only consider 50. The statement simply implies that the employee should humble and toe the line as he or she output is considered below average. An explicit threat would be if you do not improve your appraisal score, you are likely to be dropped.

Defending oneself against threats requires invoking your rights as an employee. Employees are protected against threats and one should have a basic understanding of threats and make the offending person understand that your dignity is protected against the law. However, it is important to ensure that your productivity and behavior is in line with the guidelines of the particular organization. While you are protected against any form of threats, if you have punctuality issues then your employer still has a case even though he or she should not bully you.

An enticement is a tool of bullying behavior

Believe it or not but enticement can be used to accomplish bullying behaviour. An offending person may make you excited by offers and force you to compromise your stand and dignity. Examples of enticement as a tool of bullying behaviour include recognizing or offering rewards to employees that embrace your bullying behaviour, which in turn motivates other employees to align with your bullying behaviour as a supervisor.

Regarding ways of defending oneself against bullying behaviour, one should speak out by challenging the criteria of enticement. Every worker desires for accolades and awards but this should not be exploited to endorse bullying behaviour. If possible, one should hold the organization accountable to its code of conduct. Most organizations commit to act in an ethical manner in line with the expectations of the public.

Conclusion

In summary, the author managed to define what influence is and differentiate it from the concept of manipulation. Manipulation is considered unethical and self-serving, unlike largely ethical influence. The book went further to offer a discussion of influence in advertising, influence in religion, as well as provided knowledge of ways of ethically handling other people's emotions. Interestingly, the book offers tips and a checklist to spot and stop manipulators. A reader is helped with ways of detecting deception as well as providing tips and workout to increase self-esteem to avoid being manipulated. The read is also offered examples of manipulation in daily life and explaining how to defend from it. Lastly, the book offered a guide to dealing with bullying behaviour.

As such, the author did not just define or throw definitions but presented a concrete approach of influencing people for a person with no experience of accomplishing persuasion. In the same breath, the author presented the discussion to accommodate persons with some basic background of exerting influence in various domains of social interactions such as relationships and workplaces. Where necessary, the author gave simple, relatable and comprehensive examples of how influence and manipulation works. All these should help the reader find this book as informative, illustrative and relatable when discussing ways of one becoming an influencer.

Description

Using a concrete approach and systematic approach, the author seeks to guide a novice to an informed reader on ways of influencing ethically. The book is written in such a manner to be informative, relatable and systematic. As such the author began with the following clickable chapters in which the author helped expound on the principles of persuasion, explained how manipulation differs from influence as well as the tools and techniques used to influence. When one understands, the tools employed to convince then he or she can also prepare against the influence that he or she does not want. The following chapters capture the developments:

- The Principles of Persuasion
- Explain the difference between influence and manipulation
- The tools and techniques used to influence

Expectedly, the environment we live in affects our brain development as well as how vulnerability to influence and manipulation. In overall coming from a challenging environment increases the risk of vulnerability to manipulation. All these developments are captured here:

- Explain how the environment affects our brain development

Communication is critical in attaining influence and the reader is walked through requisite communication competencies to help him or she exerts influence. Closely related to communication competencies is the use of empathy to enhance communication and impact people. The author goes deeper to make a connection between emotional intelligence and empathy, which helps make the people highly informative. All these are meant to help people become better and are captured in the following chapters:

- Communication skills improvement and influence
- How to use empathy for better communication and influence other people
- Tips to help people become a better friend, a better parent, a better partner, better businessman or women, outlining the beliefs or mental habits that one person should cultivate to use successful negotiation methods in daily life situations.

Confident that the reader is well immersed in what amounts to influence, the author begins guiding the reader on ways of exerting influence in relationships, friendship, and workplace and religion domains among others. The author separated these domains into individual chapters to enable give specific tips and techniques of exerting influence in the mentioned domains. The following chapters fully capture all these developments.

- Influence in dating and relationships

- Influence on friendship
- Influence in parenting
- Influence at workplace
- Influence in advertising
- Influence on religion

The book goes further to give ways of handling the emotions of other people and the author invokes emotional intelligence competencies to help the reader safely navigate challenging emotions such as anger exhibited by a friend. Closely related to this, the author helps the reader understand the attributes of manipulators as well as give recommendations for handling manipulators. The following chapters capture all these developments.

- Ethically dealing with other people's emotions.
- Tips and checklist to spot and stop manipulators.
- How to detect deception

We all agree that influencing people requires one to exude confidence and there is an entire chapter dedicated to ways of increasing self-esteem. Having a requisite threshold of self-esteem also helps one avoiding being manipulated. In the last two chapters, the author gives examples of manipulation in real life and a guide to handling bullying behaviour.

- Tips and workout to increase self-esteem to avoid being manipulated
- Manipulation in daily life and explaining how to defend from it
- A guide to dealing with bullying behavior

www.ingramcontent.com/pod-product-compliance
Lightning Source LLC
Chambersburg PA
CBHW070644220526
45466CB00001B/284